Jason Oddy

Geoff Dyer's books include *Paris Trance*, *Yoga for People Who Can't Be Bothered to Do It*, *The Ongoing Moment* (winner of an Infinity Award from the International Center of Photography), and, most recently, a novel, *Jeff in Venice, Death in Varanasi*. His many prizes include a Somerset Maugham Award, the E. M. Forster Award, and a Lannan Literary Fellowship. He lives in London.

Also by Geoff Dyer

Jeff in Venice, Death in Varanasi

The Ongoing Moment

Yoga for People Who Can't Be Bothered to Do It

Anglo-English Attitudes

Paris Trance

Out of Sheer Rage

The Missing of the Somme

The Search

The Colour of Memory

Ways of Telling: The Work of John Berger

BUT BEAUTIFUL

BUT BEAUTIFUL

A BOOK ABOUT JAZZ

GEOFF DYER

•

PICADOR

FARRAR, STRAUS AND GIROUX
NEW YORK

AUTHOR'S NOTE

For the American edition I have made some small changes to the body of the text and added a few lines to update the afterword and discography.

www.picadorusa.com

Picador® is a U.S. registered trademark and is used by Farrar, Straus and Giroux under license from Pan Books Limited.

For information on Picador Reading Group Guides, please contact Picador. E-mail: readinggroupguides@picadorusa.com

Pages 154–170 had their origin in a short script commissioned by Channel 4 in England on the theme of seduction. A few paragraphs of this book first appeared in very different form in *The Guardian* and *The Independent*.

ISBN 978-0-312-42947-8

Originally published by Jonathan Cape Ltd., Great Britain

First published in the United States by Farrar, Straus and Giroux

10   9   8   7   6   5   4   3

Preface

When I began writing this book I was unsure of the form it should take. This was a great advantage since it meant I had to improvise and so, from the start, the writing was animated by the defining characteristic of its subject.

Before long I found I had moved away from anything like conventional criticism. The metaphors and similes on which I relied to evoke what I thought was happening in the music came to seem increasingly inadequate. Moreover, since even the briefest simile introduces a hint of the fictive, it wasn't long before these metaphors were expanding themselves into episodes and scenes. As I invented dialogue and action, so what was emerging came more and more to resemble fiction. At the same time, though, these scenes were still intended as commentary either on a piece of music or on the particular qualities of a musician. What follows, then, is as much *imaginative criticism* as fiction.

Many scenes have their origin in well-known or even legendary episodes: Chet Baker getting his teeth knocked out, for example. These episodes are part of a common repertory of anecdote and information—

"standards," in other words, and I do my own versions of them, stating the identifying facts more or less briefly and then improvising around them, departing from them completely in some cases. This may mean being less than faithful to the truth but, once again, it keeps faith with the improvisational prerogatives of the form. Some episodes do not even have their origins in fact: these wholly invented scenes can be seen as original compositions (though they sometimes contain quotations from the musicians concerned). For a time I worried about whether I should indicate where I had someone in this book saying something he actually said in real life. In the end, by appeal to the same principle that guided all other decisions in this book, I decided against it. Jazz musicians frequently quote from each other in their solos: whether you pick up on it or not depends on your knowledge of the music. The same thing applies here. As a rule assume that what's here has been invented or altered rather than quoted. Throughout, my purpose was to present the musicians not as they were but as they appear to me. Naturally, the distance between these two ambitions is often very great. Similarly, even when I appear to be doing so I am not describing musicians at work so much as projecting back onto the moment of the music's inception the act of my hearing it thirty years later.

The Afterword picks up and expands some of the concerns of the main body of the text in a more formal style of exposition and analysis. It also offers some reflections on developments in recent jazz. Although it provides a context in which the main body of the text might be seen, it is supplementary rather than integral to it.

A Note on Photographs

Photographs sometimes work on you strangely and simply: at first glance you see things you subsequently discover are not there. Or rather, when you look again you notice things you initially didn't realize were there. In Milt Hinton's photograph of Ben Webster, Red Allen, and Pee Wee Russell, for example, I thought that Allen's foot was resting on the chair in front of him, that Russell was actually drawing on his cigarette, that . . .

The fact that it is not as you remember it is one of the strengths of Hinton's photograph (or any other for that matter), for although it depicts only a split second the *felt duration* of the picture extends several seconds either side of that frozen moment to include—or so it seems—what has just happened or is about to happen: Ben tilting back his hat and blowing his nose, Red reaching over to take a cigarette from Pee Wee . . .

.

Oil paintings leave even the Battle of Britain or Trafalgar strangely silent. Photography, on the other hand, can be as sensitive to sound as it is to light. Good photographs are there to be listened to as well as looked at; the better the photograph, the more there is to hear. The best jazz photographs are those saturated in the sound of their subject. In Carol Reiff's photo of Chet Baker onstage at Birdland we hear not just the sound of the musicians as they are crowded into the small stage of the frame but the background chat and clinking glasses of the nightclub. Similarly, in Hinton's photo we hear the sound of Ben turning the pages of the paper, the rustle of cloth as Pee Wee crosses his legs. Had we the means to decipher them, could we not go further still and use photographs like this to hear what was actually being said? Or even, since the best photos seem to extend beyond the moment they depict, what has just *been* said, *what is about to be said* . . .

Producers of great art are no demigods
but fallible human beings, often with
neurotic and damaged personalities.

THEODOR ADORNO

∎

We hear only ourselves.

ERNST BLOCH

BUT BEAUTIFUL

"Not as they were but as they appear to me . . ."

The fields on either side of the road were as dark as the night sky. The land was so flat that if you stood on a barn you could see the lights of a car like stars on the horizon, pulling toward you for an hour before the red taillights ghosted slowly to the east. Except for the steady drone of the car there was no noise. The blackness was so uniform that the driver found himself thinking that no road existed until the headlights scythed a path through the wheat writhing stiffly in the shock of light. The car was like a snowplow, shoving darkness to one side, clearing a path of light . . . Feeling his thoughts slipping away and his eyelids becoming heavy, he blinked hard and rubbed one leg to keep himself awake. He kept to a steady fifty but the landscape was so huge and unchanging that the car hardly seemed to move at all, a spacecraft inching its way to the moon . . . His thoughts drifted dreamily over the fields again, he thought maybe he could risk shutting his eyes for just one lovely second—

Abruptly the car was filled with the roar of the road and the chill of the night and he was startled to realize that he had been on the verge of nodding out. Within seconds the car was full of chisel-cold air.

—Hey, Duke, close the window, I ain't sleepy no more, said the driver, glancing at the man in the passenger seat.

—Sure you're OK, Harry?

—Yeah, yeah . . .

Duke hated the cold as much as he did and needed only this assurance to wind up the window. As quickly as it had cooled down the car began to warm up again. The dry toasty warmth you got in a car with the windows shut tight, that was his favorite kind of heat in the world. Duke had said many times that the road was his home and if that was true then this car was his hearth. Sitting up front with the heater on high and the cold landscape slipping by—to both of them that was like sitting in armchairs in an old cottage and reading books around an open fire, snow falling outside.

How many miles had they traveled together like this? Harry wondered. A million? Put that together with trains and planes and you probably had a distance three or four times the length of the earth. Probably no other people in the world had spent as much time together, or traveled so far, thousands of millions of miles possibly. He'd bought the car in '49, intending just to hop around New York, but soon he was driving Duke all over the country. Several times he'd had an impulse to keep a notebook record of how far they'd traveled but always he came to thinking how he wished he'd done it right from the start and so, each time he thought of it, he gave up the idea and fell to calculating vaguely cumulative distances, remembering the countries and towns they had passed through. That was it—they didn't really visit anywhere, they passed through the whole world, sometimes arriving at a gig twenty minutes before it started and hitting the road again half an hour after it ended.

Not keeping that notebook was just about his only regret. He'd joined the band in '27, April 1927, when he was seventeen and Duke had to persuade his mom to let him go out on the road instead of returning to school, charming her and pressing her hand, smiling and saying, "Yes, of course, Mrs. Carney" to everything she said, knowing he would get his own way in the end. Course, if Duke had mentioned that it would mean spending the rest of his life on the road things might not have been as simple. Even so, looking back on it all, there was hardly a moment or a mile he regretted—especially in the years he and Duke had been driving to gigs like this. The whole world loved Duke but hardly anyone really knew him; over the years he'd got to know Duke better than anyone and that would have been payment enough—the money was a bonus practically . . .

—How we doing, Harry?

—We're OK, Duke. Hungry?

—My stomach's been growling since Rockford. How about you?

—I'm OK. I've been saving that fried chicken I picked up yesterday morning.

—That's gonna be real tasty by now, Harry.

—Soon be time to stop for breakfast anyhow.

—Soon?

—About two hundred miles from now.

Duke laughed. They counted time in miles, not hours, and had gotten so used to huge distances that a hundred miles often elapsed between needing a leak and stopping to take one. Two hundred regularly lay between the first pangs of hunger and actually stopping to eat—and even when they came across the only place in fifty miles they often drove on anyway. Stopping was something you looked forward to so much that you could barely bring yourself to do it: a treat that had to be indefinitely postponed.

—Wake me up when we get there, said Duke, arranging his hat as a pillow between the edge of the seat and the door.

It was the quiet time of the evening, between the day people heading home from work and the night people arriving at Birdland. From his hotel window he watched Broadway grow dark and greasy with halfhearted rain. He poured a drink, piled a stack of Sinatra records on the turntable . . . touched the unringing phone and drifted back to the window. Soon the view fogged over with his breath. Touching the hazy reflection like it was a painting, his finger traced wet lines around his eyes, mouth, and head until he saw it turning into a drippy skull-shaped thing that he wiped clear with the heel of his hand.

He lay down on the bed, making only a slight dip in the soft mattress, convinced he could feel himself shrinking, fading to nothing. Scattered over the floor were plates of food he had pecked at and left. He'd take a bite of this, a little of that and then head back to the window. He ate almost nothing but he still had his preferences when it came to food: Chinese was his favorite, that was the food he didn't eat most of. For a long time he'd lived on buttermilk and Cracker Jack but he'd even lost his taste for these. As he ate less he drank more: gin with a sherry chaser, Courvoisier and beer. He drank to dilute himself, to thin himself down even more. A few days ago he'd cut his finger on an edge of paper and was surprised how red and rich his blood was, expecting it to be silver as gin, flecked with red, or pale, pinkish. That same day he'd been fired from a gig in Harlem because he hadn't had the strength to stand. Now even lifting the horn exhausted him; it felt like it weighed more than him. Even his clothes did probably.

Hawk went the same way eventually. It was Hawk who made the tenor into a jazz instrument, defined the way it had to sound: big-bellied, full-throated, huge. Either you sounded like him or you sounded like nothing—which is exactly how folks thought Lester sounded with his wispy skating-on-air tone. Everybody bullied him to sound like Hawk or swap over to alto but he just tapped his head and said,

—There's things going on up here, man. Some of you guys are all belly.

When they jammed together Hawk tried everything he knew to cut him but he never managed it. In Kansas in '34 they played right through the morning, Hawk stripped down to his singlet, trying to blow him down with that big hurricane tenor, and Lester slumped in a chair with that faraway look in his eyes, his tone still light as a breeze after eight hours' playing. The pair of them wore out pianists until there was no one left and Hawk walked off the stand, threw his horn in the back of his car, and gunned it all the way to St. Louis for that night's gig.

Lester's sound was soft and lazy but there was always an edge in it somewhere. Sounding like he was always about to cut loose, knowing he never would: that was where the tension came from. He played with the sax tilted off to one side and as he got deeper into his solo the horn moved a few degrees further from the vertical until he was playing it horizontally, like a flute. You never got the impression he was lifting it up; it was more like the horn was getting lighter and lighter, floating away from him—and if that was what it wanted to do he wouldn't try to hold it down.

Soon it was a straight choice: Pres or Hawk, Lester Young or Coleman Hawkins—two approaches. They couldn't have sounded or looked more different but they ended up the same way: swilled out and fading away. Hawk lived on lentils, booze, and Chinese food and wasted away, just like Pres was doing now.

.

He was disappearing, fading into the tradition before he was even dead. So many other players had taken from him that he had nothing left. When he played now cats said he limped along after himself, a pale imitation of those who played like him. At a gig where he'd played badly a guy came up to him and said, "You're not you, I'm you." Everywhere he went he heard people sounding like him. He called everyone else Pres because he saw himself everywhere. He'd been thrown out of the Fletcher Henderson band for not sounding enough like Hawk. Now he was being thrown out of his own life for not sounding enough like himself.

Nobody could sing a song or tell a story on the horn the way he could. Except there was only one story he played now and that was the story of how he couldn't play anymore, how everyone else was telling his story for him, the story of how he'd ended up here in the Alvin, looking out the window at Birdland, wondering when he was going to die. It was a story he didn't quite understand and one he wasn't even that motherfuckin interested in anymore except to say it began with the army. Either it began with the army or it began with Basie and ended with the army. Same either way. He'd ignored his draft papers for years, relying on the band's zigzagging itinerary to keep him five or six steps ahead of the military. Then, as he was walking off the stand one night, an army official with a sharkskin face and aviator shades came up to him like a fan asking for his autograph and handed him his call-up papers.

He'd turned up to his induction board so wasted the walls of the room shivered with fever. He sat opposite three grim military officials, one of whom never raised his eyes from the files in front of him. Knuckle-faced men who each day subjected their jaws to shaving as though they were boots to be polished. Smelling sweetly of cologne, Pres stretched out his long legs, assuming a position as close to horizontal as the hard chair permitted, looking as though he might at any moment rest his dainty shoes on the desk facing him. His answers danced around their questions, nimble and slurred at the same time. He took a pint of gin from an inside pocket of his double-breasted jacket and one of the officers snatched it from him, blaring angrily as Pres, serene and bewildered, waved slowly:

—Hey, lady, take it easy, there's plenty for everyone.

Tests showed he had syphilis; he was drunk, stoned, so wired on amphetamines his heart was ticking like a watch—and yet somehow he passed the medical. It seemed they were determined to waive everything in order to get him into the army.

Jazz was about making your own sound, finding a way to be different from everybody else, never playing the same thing two nights running. The army wanted everyone to be the same, identical, indistinguishable, looking alike, thinking alike, everything remaining the same day after day, nothing changing. Everything had to form right angles and sharp edges. The sheets of his bed were folded hard as the metal angles of his locker. They shaved your head like a carpenter planing a block of wood, trying to make it absolutely square. Even the uniforms were designed to remold the body, to make square people. Nothing curved or soft, no colors, no silence. It seemed almost unbelievable that in the space of a fortnight the same person could suddenly find himself in so totally different a world.

He had a slack, drawling walk and here he was expected to march, to tramp up and down the parade ground in boots heavy as a ball and chain. Marching until his head felt brittle as glass.

—Swing those arms, Young. Swing those arms.

Telling *him* to swing.

He hated everything hard, even shoes with leather soles. He had eyes for pretty things, flowers and the smell they left in a room, soft cotton and silk next to his skin, shoes that hugged his feet: slippers, moccasins. If he'd been born thirty years later he'd have been camp, thirty years earlier he'd have been an aesthete. In nineteenth-century Paris he could have been an effete fin de siècle character but here he was, landlocked in the middle of a century, forced to be a soldier.

■

When he woke the room was filled with the green haze of a neon sign outside that had blinked to life while he slept. He slept so lightly it hardly even merited the name of sleep, just a change in the pace of things, everything floating away from everything else. When he was awake he sometimes wondered if he was just dozing, dreaming he was here, dying in a hotel room . . .

His horn lay next to him on the bed. On a bedside cabinet were a picture of his parents, bottles of cologne, and his porkpie hat. He'd seen a photograph of Victorian girls wearing hats like that, ribbons hanging down. Nice, pretty, he thought, and had worn one ever since. Herman Leonard had come to photograph him once but ended up leaving him out of the picture altogether, preferring a still life of the hat, his sax case, and cigarette smoke ascending to heaven. That was years ago but the photo was like a premonition that came closer to being fulfilled with each day that passed as he dissolved into the bits and pieces people remembered him by.

He cracked the seal of a new bottle and walked back to the window, one side of his face dyed green in the neon glow. It had stopped raining, the sky had cleared. A cold moon hung low over the street. Cats were turning up at Birdland, shaking hands and carrying instrument cases. Sometimes they looked up toward his window and he wondered if they saw him there, one hand waving condensation from the pane.

He went over to the wardrobe, empty except for a few suits and shirts and the jangle of hangers. He took off his trousers, hung them up carefully, and lay back on the bed in his shorts, green-tinged walls crawling with the shadow angles of passing cars.

·

—Inspection!

Lieutenant Ryan flung open his locker, peered inside, jabbed with his swagger stick—his wand, Pres always called it—at the picture taped to the inside of the door: a woman's face smiling out.

—Is this your locker, Young?

—Yes, sir.

—And did you pin this picture up, Young?

—Yes, sir.

—Notice anything about that woman, Young?

—Sir?

—Does anything strike you about that woman, Young?

—She has a flower in her hair, sir, yes.

—Nothing else?

—Sir?

—She looks to me like a white woman, Young, a young white woman, Young. Is that how she looks to you?

—Yes, sir.

—And you think it's right for a nigger private to have a picture of a white woman in his locker like that?

His eyes touched the floor. Saw Ryan's boots move even closer to him, touching his toes. A blast of breath in his nostrils again.

—You hear me, Young?

—Sir.

—You married, Young?

—Sir.

—But instead of a picture of your wife you want to have a picture of a white woman so you can think of her when you jerk off at night.

—She is my wife.

He said it as soft as possible, hoping to strip the statement of offense, but the weight of the fact gave it the defiance of contempt.

—She is my wife, *sir*.

—She is my wife, sir.

—Take it down, Young.

—Sir.

—Now, Young.

Ryan stood where he was. To get to the locker Lester walked around him like a pillar, grasped his wife's face by the ear, pulled the tape free of the gray metal until the image tore, becoming a paper bridge between his fingers and the locker. Then held it limply in his hand.

—Crumple it up . . . Now throw it in the bin.

—Yes, sir.

Instead of the adrenaline surge of power he normally experienced when humiliating recruits Ryan felt the opposite: that he had humiliated himself in front of the whole company. Young's face had been so empty of self-respect and pride, devoid of anything except hurt, that Ryan suddenly wondered if even the abject obedience of slaves was a form of protest, of defiance. He felt ugly and for that reason he hated Young more than ever. He felt something similar with women: when they began to cry, that was when the urge to hit was strongest. Earlier, humiliating Young would have satisfied him—now he wanted to destroy him. He'd never encountered a man more lacking in strength, but he made the whole idea of strength and all the things associated with it seem irrelevant, silly. Rebels, ringleaders, and mutineers—they could all be countered: they met the army head-on, played by its rules. However strong you were the army could break you —but weakness, that was something the army was powerless to oppose because it did away with the whole idea of opposition on which force depends. All you could do with the weak was cause them pain—and Young was going to get plenty of that.

•

He dreamed he was on a beach, a tide of booze advancing toward him, waves of clear alcohol breaking over him, sizzling into the sand.

•

In the morning he looked out at a sky colorless as a windowpane. A bird fluttered by and he strained his eyes to keep track of its flight before it disappeared over adjacent roofs. He'd once found a bird on a windowsill, wounded in some way he couldn't establish: something wrong with its wing. Cupping it in his hands, he'd felt the flutter-warmth of its heart and nursed it back to health, keeping it warm and feeding it grains of rice. When it showed no sign of getting its strength back he filled a saucer with bourbon and that must have done the trick—after dipping its beak in the saucer for a few days it flew away. Now whenever he saw a bird he always hoped it would be the one he had taken care of.

How long ago was it that he'd found the bird? Two weeks? Two months? It seemed like he'd been here at the Alvin for ten years or more, ever since he got out of the stockade and out of the army. Everything had happened so gradually that it was difficult to establish the point at which this phase of his life had begun. He'd once said that there were three phases in his playing. First he'd concentrated on the upper range of the horn, what he called alto tenor. Then the middle range—tenor tenor—before moving down to baritone tenor. He remembered saying that but he couldn't fix in his mind when the various phases had been because the periods of his life they coincided with were also a blur. The baritone phase coincided with his withdrawal from the world, but when had that begun? Gradually he'd stopped hanging out with the guys he played with, had taken to eating food in his room. Then he had stopped eating altogether, seeing practically no one and hardly leaving his room unless he had to. With every word addressed to him he shrank from the world a little further until the isolation went from being circumstantial to something he had internalized—but once that happened he realized it had always been there, the loneliness thing: in his playing it had always been there.

Nineteen fifty-seven, that was when he'd gone to

pieces completely and ended up in Kings County Hospital. After that he'd come here to the Alvin and abandoned interest in everything except gazing out of the window and thinking how the world was too dirty, hard, noisy, and harsh for him. And booze, booze at least made the world glisten at the edges a little. He'd been in Bellevue in '55 for his drinking but he remembered little about either Bellevue or Kings apart from a vague feeling that hospitals were like the army except you didn't have to do all the work. Even so there was something nice about lying around feeling weak and having no urge to get up. Oh yeah, and one other thing. It was in Kings that a young doctor from Oxford, England, had read him a poem, "The Lotos-Eaters," about some cats who roll up at this island and decide to stay there getting high and doing nothing. He'd dug its dreamy cadences, the slow and lazy feel it had, the river drifting like smoke. The guy who wrote it had the same sound that he had. He couldn't remember his name but if anybody had ever wanted to record it, he'd have dug playing on it, playing solos between the verses. He thought of it a lot, that poem, but couldn't remember the words, just the feel of it, like someone humming a song without really remembering how it went.

That was in 1957. He remembered the date but that got him nowhere. The problem was remembering how long ago 1957 was. Anyway, it was all very simple really: there was life before the army, which was sweet, then there was the army, a nightmare from which he'd never woken up.

·

Exercises in the daybreak cold, men shitting in front of each other, food that made his stomach heave before he even tasted it. Two guys fighting at the foot of his bed, one of them pounding the other's head on the floor until blood spotted his sheets, the rest of the barracks going wild around them. Cleaning out the rust-colored latrine, the smell of other men's shit on his hands, retching into the bowl as he cleaned it.

—It's not clean, Young, lick it clean.

—Yes, sir.

At night he flopped into bed exhausted but unable to sleep. He stared at the ceiling, the aches in his body leaving splotches of purple and red in his eyes. When he slept he dreamed he was back on the parade ground, marching through what remained of the night until the clang of the noncom's swagger stick against the foot of his bed split his sleep like an ax.

He got loaded as often as he could: homemade alcohol, pills, grass, anything he could get his hands on. If he got high first thing in the morning the day slurred past like some whitewater dream that was over before he knew what had happened. Sometimes he almost wanted to laugh in spite of his fear: grown men acting out the fantasies of little boys, men who hated the fact the war was over and were determined to carry it on any way they could.

—Young!

—Yes, sir.

—You ignorant nigger cocksucker bastard.

—Yes, sir.

Oh, it was so ridiculous. However hard he tried he couldn't fathom what purpose it was meant to serve, this being shouted at continuously . . .

—Is that a smile, Young?

—No, sir.

—Tell me something, Young. You a nigger or you just bruise easy?

—Sir?

Yelling, orders, commands, insults, and threats—a delirium of open mouths and raised voices. Everywhere you looked there was a yelling mouth, a huge pink tongue flexing in it like a python, sparks of saliva flying everywhere. He liked long, tulip-stemmed phrases and in the army it was all short-back-and-sides shouts. Voices approached the condition of a baton rapped against metal. Words bunched themselves into fists, knuckle-vowels thudded into his ears: even speech was a form of bullying. When you were not marching there was the sound of others marching. At night his ears rang with the memory of slammed doors and stamping heels. Everything he heard was like a form of pain. The army was a denial of melody and he found himself thinking what a relief it would be to be deaf, to hear nothing, to be blind, numb. Senseless.

Outside his unit's quarters were tiny strips of garden where nothing grew. Everywhere was concrete except for these narrow strips of stony soil and they existed only to be kept absolutely free of any kind of plant life. To grow here a flower would have to be ugly and hard as old metal. He began to think of a weed as something beautiful as a sunflower.

Tin skies, asbestos clouds. Birds avoided flying over the barracks. Once he saw a butterfly and wondered about it.

•

He left the hotel and walked to a cinema where *She Wore a Yellow Ribbon* was playing. He had already seen it but that made no difference—he had probably seen every Western ever made. The afternoon was the worst part of the day and a movie swallowed up a good part of it in one gulp. At the same time he didn't want to spend the afternoon in the dark watching movies set at night, gangster movies or horror films. In Westerns it was always afternoon, so he was able to avoid the afternoon and get a nice helping of it at the same time. He liked to get high and let the images float before his eyes like the nonsense they were. He'd sit with the old and the infirm, unsure of who were deputies and who were outlaws, indifferent to everything on the screen except for the bleached landscape and stagecoach clouds hauling their way across sand-blue skies. He couldn't have made it through the day without Westerns but all the time he was watching them he was eager for them to end, impatient for the whole charade of settled scores to be over with so that he could emerge again into the fading daylight.

It was raining when the film ended. As he walked slowly back to the Alvin, he saw a newspaper in the gutter, his picture on one of the pages. It soaked up rain like a sponge, the paper drifting apart from itself, his picture bloating with damp, words showing through his face until it turned to gray mush.

■

In the hospital after injuring himself during training he was interviewed by the head of neuropsychology: a doctor but a soldier too, used to dealing with boys whose brains had been blasted apart by what they'd seen in combat, his sympathy severely curtailed when it came to noncombat problems. He listened curtly to Young's shambolic, nonsensical answers, convinced he was a homosexual but offering a more complex diagnosis in his report: "Constitutional psychopathic state manifested by drug addiction (marijuana, barbiturates), chronic alcoholism, and nomadism . . . A purely disciplinary problem."

As an afterthought, as if in summary, he added: "Jazz."

■

They walked out of the bar together, Lady in her white fur, clutching his arm like a cane. She was living in a place on Central Park, alone except for her dog, the blinds closed so only filtered daylight could get through. One time he had been there and watched her feed her dog from a baby's bottle. He watched her with tears in his eyes, not because he felt sorry for her, but because he felt sorry for himself and the bird that had flown away and left him. She listened to her old records to hear Lester, just as Lester played them to hear her.

Tonight was the first time he had seen anyone in he didn't know how long. No one spoke to him anymore, no one understood what he said except Lady. He'd invented his own language in which words were just a tune, speech a kind of singing—a syrup language that sweetened the world but which was powerless to keep it at bay. The harder the world appeared, the softer his language became, until his words were like beautifully cadenced nonsense, a gorgeous song that only Lady had the ears to hear.

They stood at the street corner, waiting for a taxi. Taxis—she and Lester had probably spent more of their lives in taxis and buses than most people spent in their homes. The traffic lights hung like beautiful Christmas lanterns: perfect red, perfect green in a blue sky. She pulled him closer until her face was shadowed by the brim of his hat and her lips touched the side of his face. Their relationship depended on these little touches: lips pecking each other, a hand on the other's elbow, holding his fingers in her hands as if they were no longer substantial enough to risk firmer contact. Pres was the gentlest man she had ever known, his sound was like a stole wrapped around bare shoulders, weighing nothing. She'd loved his playing more than anyone else's and probably she loved him more than anyone. Perhaps you always loved people you never fucked more purely than anyone else. They never promised you anything but every moment was like a promise about to be made. She looked at his face, spongelike and gray-tinged from drink, and wondered if their lives had had the seeds of ruin in them from birth, a ruin they had cheated for a few years but could never evade. Booze, junk, prison. It wasn't that jazz musicians died young, they just got older quicker. She'd lived a thousand years in the songs she had sung, songs of bruised women and the men they loved.

A cop walked by and then a plump tourist who hesitated, stared again, made up his mind to speak, and asked her in a German accent if she was Billie Holiday.

—You are one of the two greatest singers of this century, he announced.

—Oh, only one of two? Who's the other?

—Maria Callas. It is a tragedy that you have not sung together.

—Why, thank you.

—And you must be the great Lester Young, he said, turning to Lester. The President, the man who learned to whisper on the tenor when everyone wanted to shout.

—Ding-dong, ding-dong, said Lester, smiling.

The man looked at him for a second, cleared his throat, and produced an airmail envelope on which they both scribbled their names. Beaming, he shook their hands, wrote his address on another envelope, and told them they were always welcome in Hamburg.

—Europe, said Billie, watching him waddle down the street.

—Europe, said Lester.

A taxi pulled up just as it began to rain. Lester kissed Lady and helped her inside, waving to her as the taxi moved out again into the moving lights of traffic.

A few blocks from the hotel he stepped out into the road and cars swarmed through him like he was a ghost. As it was happening he had no idea of what was going on but, once he had reached the opposite sidewalk, he remembered the driver's eyes widened in horror, screaming brakes, a hand wedged on the horn until the car sailed through him as if he were not there at all.

•

At the court-martial he felt relaxed: whatever happened could not be worse than what he had already experienced—if he was such a problem why not just boot him out? A dishonorable discharge would be fine by him. A psychiatrist described him as a constitutional psychopath, unlikely ever to become a satisfactory soldier. Lester found himself nodding, almost smiling: oh yes he had eyes, big eyes for that.

Then it was Ryan's turn in the witness box, standing like he had a rifle and bayonet up his ass, detailing the circumstances of Young's arrest. Lester didn't bother listening: his own recollection of events was clear as moonlight gin. It was after an assignment at battalion headquarters and he was delirious with tiredness, indifferent to everything, so worn out and wasted he was filled with a hopelessness that came close to elation. Even when he glanced up at the bloodshot walls and saw Ryan standing over him he barely took any notice, hardly even blinked, not giving a motherfuckin damn about anything.

—You look ill, Young.

—Oh, I'm just high.

—High?

—I smoked a little pot, took some uppers.

—You've got drugs on you?

—Oh yes.

—Can I see them?

—Sure. Take a helping if you like.

Clutching his papers, the lawyer for the defense heard out Ryan's story and asked,

—When did you first become aware that the defendant was under the influence of something like narcotics?

—I had suspicioned it when he first came into the company.

—What made you suspect?

—Well, his color, sir, and the fact that his eyes seemed bloodshot and he didn't react to training as he should.

Pres drifted off again. He thought of yellow light pouring into a field, blood poppies nodding in a breeze.

Next thing he knew he was in the witness box himself, standing there in his shit-colored uniform, clutching a dark Bible in his hand.

—How old are you, Young?

—I am thirty-five, sir.

His voice floated across the courtroom like a child's yacht on a blue lake.

—You are a musician by profession?

—Yes, sir.

—Had you played in a band or orchestra in California?

—Count Basie. I played with him for ten years.

To their surprise all members of the court were mesmerized by the voice, eager to hear his story.

—Had you been taking narcotics for some time?

—For ten years. This is my eleventh.

—Why did you start taking them?

—Well, sir, playing in the band we would play a

lot of one-nighters. I would stay up and play another dance and leave and that is the only way I could
keep up.

—Did any other musicians take them?

—Yes, all that I knew . . .

Taking the stand to give evidence—it was like taking
the stand to play a solo. Call and response. He could
tell he had the attention of this small, sparsely popu-
lated court—a real crowd of stiffs but they were hanging on his every word. Just like a solo, you had to tell
a story, sing them a song they wanted to hear. Everyone
in the court was looking at him. The harder they concentrated on what he was saying, the slower and more
quietly he spoke, leaving words hanging, pausing in
mid-sentence, the singsong of his voice charming
them, holding them. Their attention suddenly seemed
so familiar he expected to hear the clunk of glasses,
the scrunch of ice scooped from a bucket, the swirl of
smoke and talk . . .

The army lawyer was asking him now if they knew
about his drug addiction when he went before the
board.

—Well, I'm pretty sure they did, sir, because before
I went to join the army I had to take a spinal and I
didn't want to take it. When I went down I was very
high and they put me in jail and I was so high they
took the whiskey away from me and put me in a padded
cell, and they searched my clothes while I was in the
cell.

The pauses between phrases, the connections not
quite there, the voice always just behind the sense of
what he was saying. Pain and sweet bewilderment in
every word. No matter what he said, just the sound,
the way the words shaped themselves around each
other, made each member of the court feel as though
he were being spoken to privately.

—When you say you were pretty high, what do you mean by that? Do you mean the whiskey?

—The whiskey and the marijuana and the barbiturates, yes, sir.

—When you refer to being high, could you explain that?

—Well, that's the only way I know to explain myself.

—When you are high, does it affect you physically?

—Oh yes, sir. I don't want to do anything. I don't care to blow my horn and I don't care to be around anybody . . .

—It affects you badly?

—Just nervous.

His voice like a breeze looking for the wind.

•

Seduced by the voice and then hating themselves for succumbing to it, they sentenced him to a year in the stockade at Fort Gordon, Georgia. Worse than the army even. When you were in the army being free meant getting out of the army; here freedom meant being back in the army. Concrete floor, iron door, metal bunk beds suspended from the wall by thick chains. Even the blankets—coarse, gray—felt like they had been woven from iron filings swept off the floor of the stockade workshop. Everything about the place seemed designed to remind you of how easy it would be to dash your brains out. The human skull felt delicate as tissue in comparison.

Slamming doors, clanging voices. The only way he could stop himself from screaming was to cry and to stop himself from crying he had to scream. Everything you did made things worse. He couldn't bear it, he couldn't bear it—but there was nothing to do but bear it. He couldn't bear it—but even saying that was a way of bearing it. He became quieter, looked no one in the eyes, tried to find places to hide but there was nowhere, so he took to trying to stay inside of himself, eyes peeping out of his face like an old man's face through the gap between curtains.

At night he lay on his bunk and looked at the fragment of night sky that angled through the tiny prison window. He heard the guy in the next bunk turn toward him, his face flaring yellow in the light of a match.

—Young? . . . Young?

—Yeah . . .

—You looking at them stars?

—Yeah.

—They ain't there.

He said nothing.

—You hear what I'm saying? They ain't there.

He reached across for the proffered cigarette, pulled deeply on it.

—They're all dead. Takes so long for the light to get from there to here by the time it does they're finished. Burnt out. You're looking at somethin that ain't there, Lester. The ones that are there, you can't see 'em yet.

He blew smoke toward the window. The dead stars hazed for a second and then brightened again.

.

He stacked records on the turntable and walked to the window, watching the low moon slip behind an abandoned building. The interior walls had been knocked down and within a few minutes he could see the moon clear through the broken windows at the front of the building. It was framed so perfectly by the window that it seemed as if the moon was actually in the building: a mottled silver planet trapped in a brick universe. As he continued watching it moved from the window as slowly as a fish—only to reappear again in another window a few minutes later, roaming slowly around the empty house, gazing out of each window as it went.

A gust of wind hunted around the room for him, the curtains pointing in his direction. He walked across the creaking floor and emptied the rest of the bottle into his glass. He lay on the bed again, gazing at the cloud-colored ceiling.

He waited for the phone to ring, expecting to hear someone break the news to him that he had died in his sleep. He woke with a jolt and snatched up the silent phone. The receiver swallowed his words in two gulps like a snake. The sheets were wet as seaweed, the room full of the ocean mist of green neon.

Daylight and then night again, each day a season. Had he gone to Paris yet or was that just his plan? Either it was next month or he'd already been there and come back. He thought back to a time in Paris, years ago, when he'd seen the Tomb of the Unknown Soldier at the Arc de Triomphe, the inscription 1914–18—how sad it still made him feel, the thought of someone dying as young as that.

Death wasn't even a frontier anymore, just something he drifted across in the course of walking from his bed to the window, something he did so often he didn't know which side of it he was on. Sometimes, like someone who pinches himself to see if he is dreaming, he felt his own pulse to see if he was still alive. Usually he couldn't find any pulse at all, not in his wrist, chest, or neck; if he listened hard he thought he could hear a dull slow beat, like a muffled drum at a funeral in the distance or like someone buried underground, thumping the damp earth.

The colors were slipping from things, even the sign outside was a pale residue of green. Everything was turning white. Then he realized: it was snow, falling to the sidewalk in huge flakes, hugging the branches of trees, laying a white blanket over parked cars. There was no traffic, no one out walking, no noise at all. Every city has silences like this, intervals of repose when—if only for one moment in a century—no one is speaking, no telephones are ringing, when no TVs are on and no cars are moving.

As the hum of traffic resumed he played the same stack of records and returned to the window. Sinatra and Lady Day: his life was a song coming to an end. He pressed his face against the cold of the windowpane and shut his eyes. When he opened them again the street was a dark river, its banks lined with snow.

Duke woke as they crossed the state line. He blinked, ran his hand through his hair, and looked out at the unchanged darkness of the landscape. The remains of a dream were melting in his head, filling him with a vague sadness. He eased himself in his seat, groaning at the slight ache in his back.

—Lights, he said, groping in his back pocket for something to write on. Harry reached forward and clicked on the interior light, filling the car with a pale glow that made the night and road seem even darker than before. Duke hunted along the dashboard for a pen and jotted a few things in the borders of a curling menu. He had written more hours of music than any other American and most of it began like this, scrawled on anything that came to hand: serviettes, envelopes, postcards, cardboard ripped from cereal packets. His sheet music started out like that and that was also how it ended up: original scores wound up in the bin as mayo-and-tomato-smeared sandwich wrappers after a couple of rehearsals, the essentials of the music handed over to the safekeeping of the band's collective memory.

As his pen hovered over the menu his concentration

intensified as if he was remembering something from the dream and was trying to focus the memory a little clearer. He'd been dreaming of Pres, his last years, when he was staying in the Alvin, no longer interested in remaining alive. Instead of Broadway the hotel in the dream was surrounded by a winter countryside, snow. He noted down what he could remember of the dream, nursing a semi-hunch that there was something in it he could use in a piece he'd been thinking about recently, a suite covering the history of the music. He'd done something like it before—Black, Brown and Beige—but this was going to be something specifically about jazz. Not a chronicle and not even history really, something else. He worked from small pieces, things that came to him quickly. His big works were patchworks of smaller ones and what he had in mind now was a series of portraits, not of people he'd known necessarily . . . He didn't know exactly what he was trying to get at but he could feel the idea fidgeting around inside him like a mother feels the first kick of the child in her womb. He had plenty of time—he always had plenty of time until he was about to run out of time, until a week before the premiere of whatever it was he'd been trying to write. A deadline was his inspiration, never having enough time was his muse. Some of his best pieces had been written when he was hurtling toward a deadline like someone rushing to catch a plane. "Mood Indigo" took fifteen minutes while his mother finished cooking dinner; "Black and Tan Fantasy" had come to him in a couple of minutes in the back of a taxi on his way to the studio after an all-night drinking session. "Solitude" took all of twenty minutes, scribbled standing up at the studio when he found he was a song short . . . Yeah, there was nothing to worry about, he had plenty of time.

He made notes until there was no room left on the menu, then squeezed a few lines between Appetizers and

Entrées before tossing everything back onto the dash-board.

—OK, Harry.

Carney clicked off the light and their faces were lit once again only by the faint flicker of the dials: the speedometer constant at fifty, the fuel gauge half full.

He didn't like new things. Like a blind man, he preferred stuff he'd used for a long time, even small things like pens or knives, things he'd come to feel at home with.

Walking with him one afternoon, we were waiting for the lights to change at a street corner near his place—we were always near his place. He rested his hand against a lamppost, patting it affectionately:

—My favorite lamppost.

Everyone in the neighborhood knew him. Walking to the shops, kids called out, Hey, Monk, how ya doin? Where ya bin, Monk? and he mumbled something back, stopping to shake hands or just sway back and forth on the sidewalk. He enjoyed being recognized like this—not a fame thing but a way of enlarging his home.

•

He and Nellie moved into an apartment in the West Sixties and stayed there, with their children, for thirty years. Twice fires forced them to move out and twice they moved back. Most of the space was taken up with a Baby Steinway, jammed halfway into the cooking area as though it were a piece of kitchen equipment. When he played his back was so close to the stove it looked like he might catch fire. Even if he was composing it made no difference what kind of bedlam was going on around him. He'd be working on some really tricky piece with kids crawling in and out of the piano legs, radio playing loud country music, Nellie cooking dinner while he worked away serene as if he was in the cloisters of some old college.

.

—Nothing made any difference to him, long as no one messed with him or Nellie; didn't care if no one heard his music, long as he was playing it. For six years, after he got busted for possession and lost his cabaret card, that room was practically the only place he did play.

.

He and Bud Powell were in a car, got pulled over by the police. Bud was the only one with anything on him but he froze, sat there clutching the folded paper of heroin. Monk snatched it from him and sent it butterflying out the window, landing in a puddle and floating there like a little origami yacht.

Monk and Bud sat and watched the red and blue lights from the prowl car helicoptering around them, rain sweating down the white glare of the windshield, the metronome flop of wipers. Bud rigid, holding himself barbed-wire tight. You could hear the sweat coming off him. Monk already ahead of everything, just waiting for it to happen, seeing the rain-black shapes of police lurching toward them in the rearview mirror, keeping his breath steady. A flashlight shined into the car, Monk eased himself out, a puddle clutching at his

foot and then flattening itself down again like someone
shocked briefly out of sleep.

—What's your name?

—Monk.

—You got ID?

Monk's hand moved toward his pocket—

—Steady, motioned the cop, loving the threat of saying it slow like that.

Handed him a wallet with the cabaret card, the
photo on it so dark he could have been anyone. He
glanced at Bud in the car, his eyes full of rain and
lights.

—Thelonious Sphere Monk. That you?

—Yeah. The word came clear of his mouth like a
tooth.

—Big name.

Rain falling into pools of blood neon.

—And who's that in the car?

—Bud Powell.

Taking his time, the cop bent down, picked up the
stash of heroin, peered into it, dabbed a little on his
tongue.

—This yours?

He looked at Bud, shivering in the car, looked back
at the cop.

—This yours or his?

Monk stood there, rain falling around him. Sniffed.

—Then I guess it's yours. The cop took another look
at the cabaret card, tossed it like a cigarette into a
puddle.

—And I guess you won't be needing that for a while,
Thelonious.

Monk looked down at the rain pattering his photo,
a raft in a crimson lake.

■

Was Monk got busted but he never said nothin. Something like that, wouldn't even occur to him to rat on Bud. He knew what kind of a state Bud was in. Monk was weird, coming and going out of himself like he did, but Bud was a wreck, a junkie, an alcoholic, half the time so crazy he was like a jacket with no one inside it—no way could he have survived prison.

.

Monk did ninety days, never talked about prison. Nellie visited him, told him she was doing everything she could to get him out but mostly just sat there waiting for him to say something back to her, reading his eyes. After he got out he couldn't play in New York. The idea of ordinary work never entered his mind and by then he'd just about made himself unemployable anyway, so Nellie worked. He made a few records, played out of town a few times but New York was his city and he didn't see why he should have to leave it. Mainly he just stayed at home. Laying dead, he called it.

.

The un-years was what Nellie called them. They came to an end when he was offered a residency at the 5-Spot for as long as he wanted, as long as people wanted to see him. Nellie came most nights. When she wasn't there he got restless, tense, pausing for an extra-long time between numbers. Sometimes, in the middle of a song, he called home to see how she was, grunting, making noises into the phone that she understood as a tender melody of affection. He'd leave the phone off the hook and go back to the piano so she could hear what he was playing for her, getting up again at the end of the song, putting another coin in.

—Still there, Nellie?

—It's beautiful, Thelonious.

—Yeuh, yeuh. Staring at the phone like he was holding something very ordinary in his hand.

.

He didn't like to leave his apartment and his words didn't want to leave his mouth. Instead of coming out of his lips the words rolled back into his throat, like a wave rolling back into the sea instead of crashing onto the beach. Swallowed as he spoke, forming words reluctantly as if language were a foreign language. He made no concessions in his music, just waited for the world to understand what he was doing, and it was the same with his speech, he just waited for people to learn to decipher his modulated grunts and whines. A lot of the time he relied on a few words—shit, motherfucker, yah, nawh—but he also liked saying stuff that nobody understood. He loved big words as names for his songs—crepuscule, epistrophy, panonica, misterioso—big words that were joky too, words as difficult to get your tongue around as his music was to get your fingers around.

Some nights he'd give a little speech from the stand, the words lost in brambles of saliva.

—Hey! Butterflies faster than birds? Must be, 'cause with all the birds on the scene in my neighborhood there's this butterfly and he flies any way he wanna. Yeah. Black-and-yellow butterfly.

.

He'd started the bebop look of berets and shades but that had become a uniform like the music. When he was playing now he liked to dress in suits as sober as possible, or sports jackets, setting these off with hats that defied logic but which he made look completely ordinary—as though a "mollusk" hat worn by Asian peasants were as essential an accessory to a suit as a collar and tie.

—Did his hats have any effect on his playing?

His face filled with a huge grin:

—Nawh, haha. Well, I dunno. Maybe they do . . .

■

When someone else was soloing he got up and did his dance. He started quietly, tapping a foot, clicking his fingers, then he raised his knees and elbows, rotating, shaking his head, meandering everywhere with his arms outstretched. Always looking like he was about to fall over. He spun around and around on the spot and then lurched back to the piano, giddy with purpose. People laughed when he was dancing and that was the most appropriate reaction as he shuffled around like a bear after its first taste of strong alcohol. He was a funny man, his music was funny, and most of what he said was a joke except he didn't say much. His dancing was a way of conducting, finding a way into the music. He had to get inside a piece, till it was a part of him, internalize it, work himself into it like a drill biting into wood. Once he had buried himself in the song, knew it inside out, then he would play all around it, never inside it—but it always had that intimacy, that directness, because he was at the heart of it, he was in it. He didn't play around the tune, he played around himself.

—What is the purpose of your dancing, Mr. Monk? Why do you do it?

—Get tired of sitting at the piano.

■

You had to see Monk to hear his music properly. The most important instrument in the group—whatever the format—was his body. He didn't play the piano really. His body was his instrument and the piano was just a means of getting the sound out of his body at the rate and in the quantities he wanted. If you blotted out everything except his body you would think he was playing the drums, foot going up and down on the hi-hat, arms reaching over each other. His body fills in all the gaps in the music; without seeing him it always sounds like something's missing but when you see him even piano solos acquire a sound as full as a quartet's. The eye hears what the ear misses.

He could do anything and it seemed right. He'd reach into his pocket for a handkerchief, grab it, and play with just that hand, holding the handkerchief, mopping up notes that had spilled from the keyboard, wipe his face while keeping the melody with the other hand as though playing the piano came as easy to him as blowing his nose.

—Mr. Monk, how do you feel about the eighty-eight keys of the piano. Are they too many or too few?

—Hard enough playing those eighty-eight.

■

Part of jazz is the illusion of spontaneity and Monk played the piano as though he'd never seen one before. Came at it from all angles, using his elbows, taking chops at it, rippling through the keys like they were a deck of cards, fingers jabbing at them like they were hot to the touch or tottering around them like a woman in heels—playing it all wrong as far as classical piano went. Everything came out crooked, at an angle, not as you expected. If he'd played Beethoven, sticking exactly to the score, just the way he hit the keys, the angle at which his fingers touched the ivory, would have unsteadied it, made it swing and turn around inside itself, made it a Monk tune. Played with his fingers splayed, flattened out over the keys, fingertips almost looking like they were pointed upward when they should have been arched.

A journalist asked him about that, about the way he hit the keys.

—Hit 'em any way I feel like.

.

Technically he was a limited player in that there were all sorts of things he couldn't do—but he could do everything he wanted to, it wasn't that he was held back by his technique. Certainly no one else could play his music like he could (if you played the piano properly, there were all sorts of little things you couldn't get at) and to that extent he had more technique than anyone. Equilibrium: he could think of nothing he wanted to do and couldn't.

He played each note as though astonished by the previous one, as though every touch of his fingers on the keyboard was correcting an error and this touch in turn became an error to be corrected and so the tune never quite ended up the way it was meant to. Sometimes the song seemed to have turned inside out or to have been constructed entirely from mistakes. His hands were like two racquetball players trying to wrong-foot each other; he was always wrong-fingering himself. But a logic was operating, a logic unique to Monk: if you always played the least expected note a form would emerge, a negative imprint of what was initially anticipated. You always felt that at the heart of the tune was a beautiful melody that had come out back to front, the wrong way around. Listening to him was like watching someone fidget, you felt uncomfortable until you started doing it too.

Sometimes his hands paused and changed direction in midair. Like he was playing chess, picking up a piece, moving it over the board, hesitating and then executing a different move from the one intended—an audacious move, one that seemed to leave his whole defense in ruins while contributing nothing to his attacking strategy. Until you realized that he'd redefined the game: the idea was to force the other person to win—if you won you lost, if you lost you won. This wasn't whimsical—if you could play like this then the ordinary game became simpler. He'd got bored with playing straight-ahead bebop chess.

Or you can look at it another way. If Monk had built a bridge he'd have taken away the bits that are considered essential until all that was left were the decorative parts—but somehow he would have made the ornamentation absorb the strength of the supporting spars so it was like everything was built around what wasn't there. It shouldn't have held together but it did and the excitement came from the way that it looked like it might collapse at any moment just as Monk's music always sounded like it might get wrapped up in itself.

That's what stopped it from being whimsical: nothing makes any difference with whimsy, whimsy is for low stakes. Monk was always playing for high stakes. He took risks and there are no risks in whimsy. People think of whimsy as doing whatever you feel like—but there's less to whimsy than that. Monk did whatever he wanted, raised that to the level of an ordering principle with its own demands and its own logic.

•

—See, jazz always had this thing, having your own sound so all sorts of people who maybe couldn't have made it in other arts—they'd've had their idiosyncrasies ironed out—like if they were writers they'd not 've made it 'cause they couldn't spell or punctuate or painting 'cause they couldn't draw a straight line. Spelling and straight-line stuff don't matter necessarily in jazz, so there's a whole bunch of guys whose stories and thoughts are not like anyone else's who wouldn't've had a chance to express all the ideas and shit they had inside them without jazz. Cats who in any other walk of life wouldn't've made it as bankers or plumbers even: in jazz they could be geniuses, without it they'd've been nothing. Jazz can see things, draw things out of people that painting or writing don't see.

.

He insisted his sidemen play his music the way he wanted but he wasn't dependent on them the way Mingus was. Always it was Monk and the piano, that was really what the music was about. How well they knew his music mattered more to Monk than whether they were great soloists. His music came so natural to him that it baffled him, the idea that anyone could have trouble playing it. Unless he was demanding something beyond the physical possibilities of the instrument he assumed his sidemen should be able to play whatever he asked.

.

—Once I complained that the runs he had asked for were impossible.
—You mean they don't give you a chance to breathe?
—No, but . . .
—Then you can play 'em.
People were always telling him they couldn't play things, but once he gave them a choice—You got an instrument? Well, you wanna play it or throw it away?—they found they could play. He made it seem

stupid to be a musician and not be able to do things. Onstage he'd get up in the middle of playing something, walk over to one of the musicians, say something in his ear, sit down again and resume playing, never hurrying, wandering around the stage as his hands wandered around the tune. Everything he did was like that.

—Stop playing all that bullshit, man. Swing, if you can't play anything else play the melody. Keep the beat all the time. Just 'cause you're not a drummer doesn't mean you don't gotta swing.

One time Hawk and Trane were having trouble reading some of the parts and asked Monk for an explanation.

—You're Coleman Hawkins, right, the man who invented the tenor? And you're John Coltrane, right? The music's in the horn, between you you should be able to work it out.

Most of the time he said little to us about how he wanted us to play. We'd ask him questions two or three times and get no response, he'd be staring straight ahead as if the question were addressed to someone else, to someone else in another language. Made you realize you were asking him questions and you knew the answers all the time.

—Which of these notes should I hit?

—Hit any of 'em, he said at last, his voice a gargle-murmur.

—And here, is that C sharp or C natural?

—Yeah, one a them

He kept all his music very close to him, didn't like other people seeing it, he kept everything close to him. When he went out he liked to be wrapped up in a coat—winter was his time—and he preferred not to stray too far. At the studio he'd have his music in a little book, reluctant to let other people see it, always plunging it back into his coat pocket when he was through, locking it away.

.

During the day he walked around, wrapped up in himself, figuring out his music, watching TV or composing when he felt like it. Sometimes he paced for four or five days in a row, walking the streets at first, going south as far as Sixtieth, north as far as Seventieth, west as far as the river and three blocks east, then gradually restricting his orbit until he was walking around the block and then sticking to the rooms of the apartment, pacing nonstop, hugging the walls, never touching the piano, never sitting—then sleeping for two days straight through.

There were also days when he was stranded between things, when the grammar of moving through the day, the syntax holding events together fell apart. Lost between words, between actions, not knowing something as simple as getting through a door, the rooms of the apartment becoming a maze. The use of things eluded him, the association between an object and its function was not automatic. Entering a room, he seemed surprised that this is what a door existed for. He ate food as if he was astonished by it, as if a roll or sandwich was infinitely mysterious, like he had no recollection of the taste from last time. Once he sat through dinner, peeled an orange like he'd never seen one before, silent all the while until, looking down at the long curl of peel, he said:

—Shapes, a huge grin breaking over his face.

Other times, when he felt the world encroaching, he became very still, retreated right down inside himself. He'd sit still as an armchair, so calm he looked asleep even with his eyes open, breath moving the hairs of his beard slightly. There is footage of him sitting so still that only the drifting smoke tells you it's not a photograph. Talking to Monk anyway was like talking transatlantic, a delay in things getting through—not a split second but ten seconds sometimes, so long you had to ask a question three or four times over. If he got tense the delays in responding to stimuli of any kind got longer and longer until there was no response at all, his eyes coating over like ice on a pond. Most of the times he got into difficulties were when he was apart from Nellie or in unfamiliar surroundings. If something went wrong and he felt threatened he'd disconnect very suddenly, shut himself off like a light.

If Nellie was around when he got lost in himself like that she made sure everything was OK and waited for him to find his way out. Even then she felt good being with him as he went maybe four or five days without saying a word until he broke his speech-fast and called out:

—Nellie! Ice cream!

•

—Whatever it was inside him was very delicate, he had to keep it very still, slow himself right down so that nothing affected it. Even his pacing was a way of retaining his stillness, like a waiter on a ship at sea juggling a glass of water through all sorts of angles just to keep it upright. He'd keep pacing until what was inside him became so tired of twitching around that he could collapse exhausted. These are only guesses, it was impossible to know what was going on in his head. He looked through his glasses sometimes like an animal that's been hibernating, checking to see if it is warm enough to emerge again. He was surrounded by his home, by his eccentricities, then by his silence. One time when we'd been sitting together a couple of hours and he hadn't said anything I asked him:

—What's it like in that head of yours, Monk?

Took his glasses off, held them up to his eyes, and turned them around as if they framed the face of an optician peering into his eyes.

—Take a look. I stepped forward, put my head into the glasses, studied his eyes. Sadness, lively flecks of something.

—See anythin?

—Nope.

—Shit. Haha. Reached up and put the glasses back on his head. Lit a cigarette.

I used to ask Nellie similar things. She knew him better than anybody, so well that whatever I asked her, no matter how weird Monk was acting, she'd say,

—Oh, that's just Thelonious.

.

If he had been a janitor in an office or someone in charge of supplies at a factory, waking in the morning and coming home to eat his dinner, she would have looked after him just the same as she did when they were jetting first-class all over the world. Monk was helpless without her. She told him what to wear, helped him into his clothes on the days when he seemed too bewildered even to dress himself, when he got straitjacketed in the sleeves of his suit or lost in the intricacies of knotting his tie. Her pride and fulfillment came from making it possible for him to create his music. She was so integral to his creative well-being that she may as well be credited as co-composer for most of his pieces.

She did everything for him: checking in bags at airports, looking after his passport while he stood still as a column or whirled and shambled around, people looking at him, passing around him wondering what he was doing there, shuffling around like a down-and-out, tossing his arms out like he's throwing confetti at a wedding, wearing one of his crazy hats from some part of the world he'd just come back from. And when he was on the plane and Nellie buckled his seat belt over his overcoat, people would still be wondering who he was, the head of some African state lurching toward independence or something. There were times when Nellie looked at him and wanted to cry, not because she pitied him, but because she knew one day he would die and there was no one else like him in the world.

·

When Nellie was in the hospital he sat and smoked, watched a dusty sunset peer in through the rain-grimed windows. He glanced up at the clock hanging from the wall at a surrealist tilt. Nellie had this thing about stuff being straight; Monk preferred things crooked and to get her used to the idea he'd nailed the clock to the wall like that. Every time she looked at it it made her laugh.

He walked from room to room, stood in the places she stood, sat in her chair, looked at her lipstick and makeup, her glasses case and other stuff. Before going to the hospital she had tidied everything away. He touched the fabric of her dresses hanging neat and empty in the closet, looked at the shoes waiting for her in rows.

She did so many things for him that most objects in the apartment were a mystery to him and he saw them for the first time: the casserole dish, stained from years of use, the steam iron. He picked up her pots and pans, missing the familiar noise of their clanking together. He sat at the piano, building a tune out of all the sounds he missed as she moved around the apartment: the rustle of her clothes as she got dressed, water running in the sink, the clatter of plates. She called him Melodious Thunk and he wanted to write a song for her that sounded just like that. Every five minutes he got up and peered out of the window, checking in case she was heading up the street.

Each day when he visited her she was more worried about him than herself. He sat by the side of her bed, not speaking, smiling when the nurses asked if everything was OK. He stayed for the full duration of visiting time because there was nothing else he wanted to do.

Reluctant to return to the apartment, he walked over to the Hudson to watch the sun set over the freeway expanse of water. A famished wind snatched the smoke from his cigarette. He thought about Nellie and the song he was writing for her, a private thing for piano that no one else would touch. Once he'd written it it would be finished—he'd play it just as it was, unaccompanied with no improvising. He didn't want Nellie to change and he didn't want his song about her to change either. As he looked out across the river a smear of yellow-brown light welled up over the skyline like paint squeezed from a tube. For a few minutes the sky was a blaze of dirty yellow until the light faded and oil-spill clouds sagged again over New Jersey. He thought about heading back to the apartment but stayed on in the sad twilight and watched dark boats crawl over the water, the grief of gulls breaking over them.

.

Driving to a gig at the Comedy Store, Baltimore. With him Nica and Charlie Rouse, friends for life. Virtually everything Monk did he did for life. Pulled into a motel in Delaware. Monk was thirsty, which meant he had to have a drink. Everything was like that with him. He'd stay up three or four days straight because he didn't feel like sleep and then he'd sleep solidly for two days, anywhere. If he wanted something he had to have it. He walked into the lobby, filling the doorframe, looking dark as a shadow to the desk clerk who jumped slightly when he saw him. Unnerved not just by his blackness, his size, but by the way he ambled in there like an astronaut. Something about him, not just the eyes either, his whole bearing, looking like a statue that might fall over at any moment. And something else too. That morning the booking clerk had scouted around his apartment for clean underwear. Unable to find any, he'd put on a pair of shorts he'd already worn for three long days, blemished yellow and giving off a vague smell, he kept wondering if other people noticed. Monk happened to sniff as he came into the room and that did it, that was one of the things that did it. Maybe nothing would have happened if he'd had clean shorts, but as it was, the slight stickiness, the itch that had been there all day became unbearable when this huge colored walked in, sniffing the air like it was dirty. Immediately he said there were no rooms, before Monk had even uttered a word. Staring, wearing a crazy hat like he was a pope or cardinal in Africa.

—Saywhaman? Whatever he said lost in a saliva-strangle of sound. A voice like it was coming over the radio from Mars.

—No vacancies. I'm afraid we have no rooms.

—Tayuhglassawar.

—Water?

—Yauh.

—You want water?

Monk nodded like a sage, standing in front of the man, like he was getting in his way, obstructing his view. Something about him was making the desk clerk shake with anger. The way he was standing there, like a striker on a picket line, determined not to budge. Couldn't get a fix on him, not a hobo, dressed . . . dressed—shit, he couldn't tell rightly how he was dressed: tie, suit, coat—the clothes were smart but he looked a mess, like his shirttails were hanging out or like he was not wearing socks.

—No water, the booking clerk said finally, the words gurgling out like the first rusty belch of water from a tap suddenly twisted.

—No water, he said again, clearing his throat. He was more frightened now, the colored's yellow eyes staring at him like two planets in space. Even more unnerving was the way Monk was staring not at his eyes but at a spot two inches above them. Quickly he passed a hand over his forehead, feeling for a zit.

—No water. You hear me?

The colored stood there, like he'd turned to stone, like he'd gone into some nigger trance. He'd never seen anyone so black. Now he was thinking that the colored was maybe mentally defective in some way, dangerous, a maniac. Staring at him like that.

—You hear me, boy—he felt more confident now, as soon as he called him boy he felt the situation becoming less a specific confrontation between two individuals, more something general, like he had people on his side, backing him up, a man with a mob behind him.

—This a hotel you don't got a glassawar? Must be lot a thirsty muthafuckahs all them full rooms you got.

—Don't get smart, don't even think about getting smart—

At that moment Monk moved a step forward, blocking the light completely, becoming a silhouette; looking into his face was like stepping into a cave on a bright day.

—Now we don't want any trouble here, said the booking clerk. The word "trouble" smashed like a bottle. His chair squeaked back an involuntary inch, anxious to keep the same distance between him and this man looming over him like a cliff. Looked down at the colored's hands hanging at his side, a big cheek-ripping ring on one finger. That's when it occurred to him that if he had a gun he'd have pulled it on him —looking back on it later he realized it was this thought on his part rather than anything the colored had done that escalated the situation. Each word triggered the next. The word "trouble" pulled the word "gun" out of its holster and the word "gun" brought the word "police" hurrying after it.

—Like I said, we don't want no trouble here, so you leave quickly or I'm calling the police.

Standing there, dumb as stone, dumb like the only two words he knew were "glass" and "water." The expression on his face had changed now, like he wasn't seeing anything at all, like he didn't know where he was, no idea. Swelling up in himself like he might explode at any moment. The clerk was almost too terrified to dial the police, worried that might be the action to spring him out of whatever he was in—but doing nothing was even more frightening. Decided the way to do it was as blatantly as possible, tugging the phone over, picking the receiver up slowly, dialing like he was dipping his finger in a pot of maple syrup.

—Police? All the time he was speaking he kept one eye, both eyes, on the colored, whose only movement was the rise and fall of his chest. Breath.

—Well, he's refusing to leave. Standing there like I don't know, like he's gonna cause trouble . . . I've told him that . . . Yes, I think he might be dangerous.

He had just replaced the phone—slowly, like everything he was doing now—when another colored and some rich-looking woman came bustling into the lobby.

—Thelonious? What's happened?

Before he had a chance to speak the booking clerk intervened.

—This freak with you? His fear was subsiding, he felt confident now of his ability to goad the situation any which way he liked. The woman looked at him like he was an insect crawling along a wall. The kind of woman who wherever she went would be surrounded by lawns of privilege, even her politeness a form of contempt, the friendliness she lavished on some serving to remind others of the riches they were excluded from.

—What's going on, Thelonious?

Still not speaking, just that glare turned on the booking clerk.

—You'd better stick around, lady. The police are on their way and they'll want to ask some questions.

—What?

—Be here any minute.

By some tacit agreement the woman—sounding like the queen of England—and the other colored maneuvered him out of the lobby, back to the car. Monk had got into the driver's seat and turned the engine on just as the cops arrived, three of them clambering out of the car. The desk clerk ushered them over to the automobile, keeping in back, out of sight. A flurry of questions, the cops barely polite, not knowing what to make of it but knowing some show of nightstick authority was called for. Told him to turn off the key, the engine. He ignored them, stared straight ahead like he was concentrating hard on the road on a foggy night, unsure of the way. One of the cops reached in, twisted off the ignition himself. The English woman saying something.

—Lady, you just keep quiet. I want everybody outta the car. Him first . . . Hey, you, get outta the car.

The colored hunched over the wheel, hands perfectly positioned like he was the captain on the bridge of a ship passing through a storm.

—Listen, you fuckin deaf or somethin? Outta the car, get outta the fuckin car.

—Let me handle this, Steve.

Pushing his head close to Monk's face, the second cop spoke quietly, hissing practically.

—Hey, you dumb-ass nigger, you got about ten seconds to get outta this fuckin car before I pull you out. You hear that?

The colored sitting there, big shoulders, still wearing the crazy pope hat.

—OK, you have it your way. Instantly grabbed him by the shoulders, pulling him half out of the car, but his hands were still clinging to the steering wheel like he was handcuffed to it.

—Goddam. The cop started pulling at his wrists, which were thick, corded with muscle, immovable. The English bitch yelling, the cops yelling too.

—Lemme get at this dumb-fuck . . . Getting in each other's way, one of them drawing his nightstick and pounding it down on Monk's hands, hard and fast as he could in the confines of the car, hard enough to draw blood, making the knuckles puff up and the English woman screaming about he's a pianist, his hands, his hands . . .

■

—At the Vanguard it was packed, Monk playing solo. A couple of college students bartered with the doorman, trying to get a table right up close by the piano.

—You kidding? You get here halfway through the set and expect a table at the front. People want to see his hands, man . . .

•

At a hotel in Boston he walked around the lobby for an hour and a half, inspecting the walls, peering at them like they were pictures, running his hands over them, orbiting the room, alarming guests. Asked for a room and was told to get out before there was any trouble. Leaving the hotel, he walked the revolving doors for ten minutes, pushing patiently like a pit pony. At that night's gig he played two numbers and left the stage. An hour later he came back, played the same two songs again and then sat staring at the piano for half an hour until the band left the stage and the manager played "Who Knows" over the PA. People got up to leave, wondering if they'd seen him crack up before their eyes. No one jeered or complained, a couple of people spoke to him, touched his shoulder, but he made no response. It was as if everyone had stepped thirty years into the future into an installation entitled "Thelonious Monk at the Piano," a museum exhibit simulating the atmosphere of jazz clubs of old.

Later, in a panic dash to find Nellie and head for the airport, he was stopped by a state trooper. Frazzled by tiredness, he refused to say a word, not even his name. He slept for a long time, dreamed he was in the hospital and when he woke he found he was eating food spooned to him in bed, looking up at nurses like a man trapped beneath the rubble of a collapsed building. Lights peered into his eyes like he was an animal. Held himself close, in possession of a secret so precious he had forgotten what it was. People had been saying he was crazy for so long that he shuffled along in Lowell pajamas like someone who had been there a long time. Played a few chords on the piano and the doctors thought they noticed some untutored musical instinct twitching from his hands, hitting notes that had a kind of ugly beauty. Tinkly, thunking things. Other patients liked his playing, one howling along, another joining in with a song about a man and a faithful horse that died, a couple of others just crying or laughing.

.

Silence settled on him like dust. He went deep inside himself and never came out.
—What do you think the purpose of life is?
—To die.
He spent the last ten years of his life at Nica's place just across the river in New Jersey, a view of Manhattan filling the tall windows, lived there with Nellie and the kids too. He didn't touch the piano because he didn't feel like it. Saw no one, rarely talked or got out of bed, enjoyed simple sensations like smelling a bowl of flowers, seeing the leaves spongy with dust.

.

—I'm not sure what happened to him. It was like he was in the grip of a prolonged flinch—like something had grazed him, as if he had stepped out into traffic and a car had just missed him. He got lost inside the labyrinth of himself and puttered around there, never found a way out.
Maybe nothing happened to him externally. Only the weather in his own head was important and suddenly everything clouded over as it had many times before—but this time for ten years. It wasn't despair, almost the opposite: a form of contentment so extreme that it was almost torpor, like when you stay in bed

for a whole day, not because you can't bear to face the horror of the day, but because you don't feel like it, because it's nice lying there. Everyone has that impulse to do nothing but it rarely takes root. Monk was used to always doing what he felt like and if he felt like staying in bed for ten years he'd do that, regretting nothing, wanting nothing. He was at the mercy of himself. He had no self-discipline because he'd never needed any. He'd worked when he felt like it and now he no longer felt like it, no longer felt like anything.

.

—Yes, I would say there was a lot of sadness in him. The things that happened to him, most of it stayed in him. He let a little of that out in music, not as anger, just a bit of sadness here and there. "Round Midnight," that's a sad song.

.

Autumn in New York, a brown sludge of leaves underfoot, a light rain barely falling. Halos of mist around trees, a clock waiting to strike twelve. Almost your birthday, Monk.

The city quiet as a beach, the noise of traffic like a tide. Neon sleeping in puddles. Places shutting and staying open. People saying goodbye outside bars, walking home alone. Work still going on, the city repairing itself.

At some time all cities have this feel: in London it's at five or six on a winter evening. Paris has it too, late, when the cafés are closing up. In New York it can happen anytime: early in the morning as the light climbs over the canyon streets and the avenues stretch so far into the distance that it seems the whole world is city; or now, as the chimes of midnight hang in the rain and all the city's longings acquire the clarity and certainty of sudden understanding. The day coming to an end and people unable to evade any longer the nagging sense of futility that has been growing stronger through the day, knowing that they will feel better when they wake up and it is daylight again but knowing also that each day leads to this sense of quiet isolation. Whether the plates have been stacked neatly away or the sink is cluttered with unwashed dishes makes no difference because all these details—the clothes hanging in the closet, the sheets on the bed—tell the same story—a story in which they walk to the window and look out at the rain-lit streets, wondering how many other people are looking out like this, people who look forward to Monday because the weekdays have a purpose which vanishes at the weekend when there is only the laundry and the papers. And knowing also that these thoughts do not represent any kind of revelation because by now they have themselves become part of the same routine of bearable despair, a summing up that is all the time dissolving into the everyday. A time of the day when it is possible to regret everything and nothing in the same breath, when the only wish of all bachelors is that there was someone who loved them, who was thinking of them even if she was on the other side of the world. When a woman, feeling the city falling damp around her, hearing music from a radio somewhere, looks up and imagines the lives being led behind the yellow-lighted windows: a man at his sink, a family crowded together around a television, lovers drawing curtains, someone at his desk, hearing the same tune on the radio, writing these words.

Thunder stumbled around in the darkness. A few drops of rain splattered the windshield and then a storm engulfed them. Wind howled across the fields, pummeling the side of the car. Rain drilled the roof. Harry looked across at Duke, slumped in his seat and gazing ahead, the headlights of approaching cars splashing like fireworks in the streaming windshield. It was exactly episodes like this that found their way into his music in one way or another. Hardly any of his music came to him as music. Everything started with a mood, an impression, something he'd seen or heard which he then translated into music. Driving out of Florida, they'd heard an invisible bird call out, so perfect and beautiful you could have sworn you'd seen it silhouetted against the sun streaking red across the horizon. As always, they didn't have time to stop, so Duke made a note of the sound and used it later as the basis of "Sunset and the Mocking Bird." "Lightning Bugs and Frogs" came from the time they'd been heading out of Cincinnati and had come across tall trees backlit by a Ping-Pong moon. Lightning bugs flashed in the air and all around was the baritone croak of frogs . . . In Damascus, Duke had *woken up to an earthquake roar of cars, as if all the rush-hour traffic of the world had become snarled up in this one city; still not fully awake he'd found himself trying to orchestrate it. The light in Bombay, the sky drifting over the Arabian Sea, a filth storm in Ceylon —wherever he was, however tired, he'd note it down without pausing to consider its significance, confident he'd discover its musical potential later. Mountains, lakes, streets, women, girls, pretty women, beautiful women, views of streets, sunsets, oceans, views from hotels, members of his band, old friends . . . He'd reached the point where virtually everything he encountered found its way into his music—a personal geography of the earth, an orchestral biography of the colors, sounds, smells, food, and people—everything that he had felt, touched, and seen . . . It was like being a word writer in sound—and what he was working on was a huge musical fiction that was always being added to and which was ultimately about itself, about the guys in the band who played it . . .*

The rain eased for a few moments and then fell even harder than before. Looking through the windshield was like peering out through a waterfall. The wind shrieked like a madman. Harry gripped the wheel tight and glanced across at Duke, wondering how long it would be before this storm found its way into his work.

It's like a séance here, Bud. The lights have been turned down low, candles are burning. Pictures of you are propped all around my desk, "The Glass Enclosure" is playing quietly on the stereo. I'm sitting in this apartment on Third Street, Bud, trying to reach you through your music. For everyone else—for Pres and Mingus and Monk—the music is a trail; I follow it and always, eventually, it leads me to them, brings me close enough so that I can see them move, hear them speak. With you it's different. Your music encloses you, seals you off from me. Photographs of you have the same quality, your eyes acting like sunglasses, concealing what lies behind them. It's not so much that you seem cut off from the world, more like the world can't get close to you. Even relaxed you have the look of a man guarding something, like a farmer photographed by the fence at the edge of his property. Or like this photo of you and Buttercup and Johnny outside the sanatorium where you were treated for TB. Like all these photos of you, it was taken at the edge, the border of a season. A light rain is falling through absent trees. Your raincoat is buttoned up to the neck, your cap pulled down over your forehead, shielding your eyes; Buttercup is holding a handbag and wearing a headscarf. The three of you look like a poor family caught out by the weather on a vacation they can't afford or enjoy. You're one of those people who don't pose for a photo—you stop for it, as if the stillness of the image is dependent on your own immobility, as if the longer you hold still, the better the picture will be.

Photographs of you at the piano are something else—like this one, taken at Birdland on one of those nights when you could play anyone else off the stand —Bird, Dizzy, anybody. Taking chorus after chorus, shoulders shrugging along with the beat, eyes closed, a vein throbbing in your temple, sweat raining on the keyboard, lips stretched back over your teeth, right hand babbling and dancing like water over rock, a foot thumping out a rhythm that got stronger and stronger as the movements of the right hand got more and more intricate, melodies blooming and fading like flowers, the momentum never easing up and then gracing effortlessly into a ballad, the keys reaching up to you, competing with each other for your touch as if the piano had been waiting a hundred years for this chance to know what it felt like to be a sax or trumpet in a black man's hands. Snarling at the audience between numbers. Hearing your name whispered wherever you went: Bud Powell, Bud Powell.

Music took nothing out of you. Life did all the taking. Music is what you were given back but it wasn't enough, not nearly enough.

•

There's another picture here, taken in 1965. By then you could hardly even play a tune, the piano had become an impossible, a deranged instrument. You are straddling a chair, smiling out at the camera under your Tatum mustache, grown plump like Tatum too. You used to sit for days on end like that in your room, didn't you? Folks would come by to visit and there you'd be, not answering any questions, just smiling benignly at the world, saying nothing.

A photograph is an image held in the trance of time. Waiting for that image to thaw, to come alive, is like sitting in that room with you, waiting for you to emerge from your trance, waiting for you to move, to talk; it's like I've called around at your place, like I'm there with you.

Bud? Bud? . . . I'll do the talking for both of us if that's the way you want it. Maybe I'll learn something from watching you listen. Maybe I'll learn how to reconcile all the pain of your life with the bouncing optimism of the music, of songs like "Oblivion," "Wail," "Hallucination," "Un Poco Loco." I want everything you play to be a page torn from the tormented novel of your life—I want "The Glass Enclosure" to be your "Waking in the Blue" but instead it sounds like a symphony frozen in the shape of a little tune for piano. Even on standards your playing has that quality, the grandeur and stateliness of a concert pianist. You take a song like "Polka Dots and Moonbeams" and make it sound like the work of a court composer . . .

You sit there so quiet, Bud, I'm not even sure if you can hear what I'm saying. I know I must seem like some drunk collaring you between sets and bombarding you with questions and stories you don't want to hear, trying to tell you what you're thinking—what I think you're thinking. There are so many things I want to know but you sit there in your quietness and I don't know what else I can do except keep talking to you, answering my own questions, hoping that maybe I'll say something that might get through to you, something true enough to lure you out of your silence. I want to know about all the time you spent locked out of harm's way: ten weeks in 1945, most of 1948, and then back in only months after being released. Out again in April 1949, committed to Pilgrim State Hospital September 1951, transferred to Creedmoor until 1953. Electroconvulsive therapy, sedation . . . Checking the dates was easy—but how did it happen, Bud? No one seems to know—except that you were twenty-five—just twenty-five—when they broke you apart and after that the rest of your life was spent trying to get glued back together. Were you walking into the Savoy Ballroom in Harlem when the bouncer split your head like a melon? Or were you drunk, surrounded by cops just waiting for an excuse to bust your sweet head open? Yelling and pleading at the same time, tears at the back of your eyes, feeling the situation slipping beyond anyone's control. Walking away, striding off until a hand reached out, grabbed your arm, and spun you back into the midst of what was always about to happen. Certain events in life are like that, lying in wait for you to chance by, patient as rain.

You were wearing black shoes and a black suit, carrying an umbrella, striding into trouble like a businessman into his office. The light of a café scribbled the violent word "berserk" on a wall nearby. The gutter was already glittering with wasted glass. Sheer with threat, a voice said,

—I'm warning you.

You looked at the voice with terror in your eyes, your options closing in on you. You lashed out at the nearest face, desperate to break through the uniformed bodies crowding in. Arms grabbing at you, a fist numbing one side of your face, stumbling, regaining your balance and glimpsing an arm rising high above, high as a noose snaking over the high branch of a tree, hanging there, and then a long scream as the nightstick came down, having time to think that it is unbelievable anyone would do that, a blow to the head like that would fracture your skull, smash your brains, kill you. You saw the open mouth of one of the cops shouting,

—No no.

Your hand raised only an inch or two in the time it took the nightstick to fall, splitting your head like a flash of lightning that lasts forever, like a gun held against your skull and fired, a hammer swung at a glass window. Dropped you to your knees. One hand reached up, hanging on to the gun belt of the nearest cop, half struggling to your feet, the initial smack of impact only now spreading out through your head like the shock wave of an ax through a knotted log. No no no.

—Oh my God.

Maybe that's not the way it was but it must have been that way. Twenty years later you would wake in the hard night and feel the hurt of your skull still trying to knit itself together again. You were twenty-five when it happened, young and arrogant as a knife, demanding whatever you wanted, walking over the crisp white tablecloths at Minton's, boots stacked with mud. The waiters about to go for you except Monk calling out,

—Don't a sonabitch move.

So everyone was left standing there, watching you step over the tabletops like a boy picking his way across the stones of a pond. Perhaps you were always potentially out of control but now that potential had been unleashed. Heroin and booze. Two drinks sent you wild but you drank like a man crawling out of a desert and into a mirage. You didn't get drunk, you got deranged. Like that night in Birdland, playing with Mingus, Blakey, Kenny Dorham, and Bird. Six months earlier Bird had tried to kill himself, had been recovering in Bellevue, so this was a comeback gig, an attempt to reestablish his credibility—but he didn't even show up in time for the first set and you went onstage without him. You were legless, the keyboard pitching under your hands like a ship at sea. Tunes disintegrated halfway through, every fifth note a mistake as you played bits and pieces from any song that came into your head until you forgot that and dabbed at something else, ending up in brambles and thickets of wrong notes.

The second set: you came on alone, grinned, bowed, danced a little and almost collapsed into the audience. Somehow you made it to the piano stool, fingers drooling over the keyboard, dripping from it like booze from a spilled glass, the tune falling to the floor in puddles. Mingus and Dorham joined in but by now the piano's function was limited to stopping you from falling to the floor.

Bird appeared, loaded again. The night before, you'd come up to him, smiling and said,

—You know, Bird, you ain't shit. You don't kill me. Man, you ain't playing shit no more.

And Bird had just smiled back. Now he called the first tune—"Hallucination"—but you went on playing what you had been before he took the stage. The band shuffled to a stop. Bird announced the tune again but you went on playing like you were deaf.

—Come on, Bud.

—What key, muthafuckah?

—The key of S—key of shit, muthafuckah.

—Muthafuckin shit piece of muthafuckin . . .

With that you smashed your elbow onto the keyboard, yelled something no one could make out and reeled offstage, feet slurring behind you. Bird was standing at the microphone, his voice a low drone, saying over and over, like for a person lost in a forest:

—Bud Powell.

—Bud Powell.

—Bud Powell.

.

In Creedmoor you drew a keyboard on the wall, pounding out new chords, stubbing your fingers, leaving a score of smudged prints on the white wall. When Buttercup came to visit, you clutched her hands, looked at the love in her eyes, the love and the question that was always there: how long? Wishing you were well again and then wondering how long it would be before you got sick again. Always waiting for something to end and something else to begin, waiting for the telltale signs of breakdown, the small events that would snag in his mind . . .

Late one afternoon he glanced up and saw the shadow of a flag cast perfectly onto the top stories of a block. He looked around, expecting to see the Stars and Stripes fluttering from a nearby roof but could see nothing, only that black ripple of shadow dancing on the wall. The next day he noticed a murmur in the texture of things, a shiver in the walls of buildings. Suddenly conscious of edges, he would place a coffee cup right in the center of a table only to see it fall to the floor and smash. Saw a jackhammer pounding the road, a pneumatic drill splitting the street, a demolition ball thumping through the ribs of a building. Startled by a shadow-flock of birds skating the pavement. A few blocks further on he saw construction workers fixing the fire escape of an old block. He watched the blue-white light of the arc welder, knowing it was too bright but continuing to stare. When he looked away his vision swam with bright saucers of light. Kept waiting for these afterimages to fade but the magnesium brightness had scarred his retina, imprinted itself as a blue force, a silver flash in his head.

Gales shrieked through the city, tornadoes strafed the streets. In the meat-packing district the air was clogged with the sawdust reek of offal. Split carcasses dangling from hooks, pink and yellow sculptures of frozen meat.

Heard people calling to him, words that sharded into broken syllables. Sensed people looking at him, noticing something wrong about him, following him. Lightning flashed in bright sunlight. In the crowds of Christmas shoppers he began to pick out the faces of the dead.

A huge Santa Claus was smiling and rattling a can in his face. Window displays were bright with presents for the dead. Someone touched his arm and he looked around and saw Art Tatum grinning at him, saying words to him he didn't understand. Tatum guided him by the arm as if he were blind, turning off the avenue into a street where there was so little traffic that the snow had settled even on the road.

—You're dead, man, you're dead, he said to Tatum suddenly, and Tatum laughed.

—Sure.

They walked down the icy steps leading to a basement bar, its lights yellowing the pavement snow. Inside, the bar was lit by amber lanterns. Colored streamers and decorations hung from the ceiling, the bar posts were ivied with gold tinsel. He followed Tatum through the crowded smoke. Everyone in the bar recognized him and called out his name, asked when he got into town and was he gonna play? Shouts and whoops from the audience punctuated a shrieking trumpet on a stage he couldn't see. As his eyes got used to the fog of yellow light he recognized Buddy

Bolden, King Oliver, Fats Waller, Jelly Roll Morton. Folks at the bar made way for Tatum, who ordered drinks and passed them back to him. Tatum was saying, later, later, to everyone who asked if he was going to play, accepting beers from whoever offered to buy one.

—Am I dead, Art? Bud said in Tatum's ear.

—Well, it's more like you've reached the stage where you don't have to worry no more about dying because that's already happened.

—How come I don't feel dead?

—Nobody feels dead here.

He saw Bolden coming toward him, embracing Tatum and then turning toward him, beaming and saying,

—Bud Powell, right? Pumping his hand and slapping his shoulder. He'd never seen a photograph of Bolden but he knew it was him. All around people were looking at him and nodding as if this were a bar he had been going to for twenty years. Bolden introduced him to King Oliver and soon he had forgotten that everyone in the bar was dead, abandoning his surprise as though it were a prejudice. It was like being in a place where everyone was white but no one took any notice of your color and soon you stopped even being aware of it, stopped even noticing that you were in a bar where there were no living people.

.

Out in the street again burnt-out buildings reared up like a tidal wave of masonry. Shadows coiled around him. He caught a glimpse of himself in the red and silver lights of a store. Wondering if he were made of glass, he kicked at the window, saw his reflection shiver and frost until there was a slow drizzle of glass and his face lay in pieces on the floor. Rain began to fall and soon a storm was raging silently around him. Hail drilled the noiseless streets. He saw the welcome lights of a liquor store, the yellow rain of taxis gliding down the street, quieter than a silent movie where every frame is filled with the din of chase. New York was probably the noisiest place on earth and he could hear nothing. He saw a car slide quietly into the back of another, saw the two drivers get out and dance silently in front of each other, aping the gestures of rage. A spasm of lightning drenched the street. He stepped off the edge of the sidewalk into a gasoline lake of rain. Around his ankles curled the barbed wire of hail exploding as silently as the image of a star-filled night on the thin ice of a lake. He could feel the wind and the rain stinging his face but there was no sound—as if the wind and rain were not external things but a strange reaction of his skin to something happening deep within him. A taxi ghosted through the steam that gushed from the cracked street. A prowl car drifted by, the rain scythed by the red and blue swirl of light.

In Central Park it rained and stopped raining. Clouds surfed past the moon, silver shadows crawled the dark grass. Lightning and then the long wait for thunder that never came. A bright moon smoldered through the hydra branches of trees. The only sound he could hear was the thump of his heart: a steady bass increasing in tempo as he moved faster and faster until he was running. He saw a shivering dog, took the shirt from his back, and helped the dog put its front legs through the sleeves, buttoning it around his belly, wrapping his trousers around the dog's throat like a college scarf. Pulled socks on his paws, tying them with the laces from his shoes, and watched the dog pad off into the night. The lake was in his way, so he floated across, keeping his head beneath the surface until the sound of his heart became loud as a bass drum, climbing out the other side like a monster emerging from the sea. Lightning blasted a tree in two. He lay down in the seaweed mush of grass, looked at the lights of the buildings, the planes gliding through the air, quieter even than on the first day of creation, before there were any cities, before there was any wind, when the only music was the beating of God's heart. He was going to live here, he'd eat dogs or cats, trees if necessary. In the fall he'd eat fallen leaves, live in a trash can or the inside of a tree.

■

Huddled in a doorway, seeing the flashlight encroaching on him, the boots getting nearer. Pistol, nightstick, heavy boots, handcuffs. Fleeing rats. The flash touched his toes and then the silver light slashed straight in his eyes and he flinched back further into the retreating army smell of old garbage, shielding his eyes. He was naked except for underwear and the pages of old newspaper that briefly mentioned his disappearance. There were cuts on his face he could remember nothing about and he was ready now for another beating as the light struck his head again.

—Easy, easy. Instinctively the patrolman lapsed into the language he might adopt if speaking to an animal that had become lost. His light revealed a youngish colored, eyes like he's seen something so terrible he can never get over it.

—Easy, easy, he said again, careful to keep the torch light away from his eyes. He moved some of the garbage out of the way with his boot and moved a little closer to the huddled figure.

—Nobody's gonna hurt you. You OK? You been hurt?

He scanned his body with the flashlight, could see no discernible signs of injury except a few cuts.

—Look, I'm not gonna hurt you, I'm not gonna book you for anything, OK? You understand. You got a name? . . . You don't got a name? He was shaking his head but looked less frightened now; even if he couldn't understand what was said the tone of the cop's voice reassured him.

By now the patrolman was crouched down beside him, a hand resting on his shoulder, allowing the streetlight to illuminate the face before him. He clicked off the flashlight, looked again at the heavily lidded eyes, the mustache, the hair that looked unruly even though it was close-cropped. Without any conscious thought he was suddenly sure the person in front of him was Bud Powell. Jesus, it couldn't be. Four hours before he came on duty he was listening to "Dance of the Infidels," telling his wife how Bud had to be the greatest pianist in the world. It couldn't be . . . but he knew Bud was schizophrenic, that he'd gone missing a few days previously. He looked again at the colored guy's face, the eyes revealing nothing except the gradual diminution of fear. Yes. Shit yes, it was him.

—You're Bud Powell, aren't you? he said at last, the tone of his voice changing from tenderness to reverence.

Bud looked at him, said nothing, but there was relief at the back of his eyes, like when you knock on someone's door at night and a light comes on in a distant room, something you feel as much as see. As he reached for Bud's hand, partly to help him up and partly just to shake it, he could not help smiling and blurting out,

—This is the greatest day of my life, Bud, I mean it . . .

．

All mental institutions were the same, secretive Victorian buildings where the apparatus of healing was indistinguishable from the equipment of punishment. A prison, a madhouse, a barracks—each could be instantly converted into the other. A course of treatment was a course of correction. Every building was a potential asylum.

.

He left the asylum on a clear late-autumn morning, noticing the crunch of gravel under his feet, the waiting car. A photographer took a picture of him standing side by side with his manager. He looked at the camera like it wasn't there, giving it nothing, holding everything in, waiting for the photograph to be over with.

He sniffed the air, empty except for the chucked rags of departing birds. He saw his face staring up at him from a puddle, the reflected sky deep as space. He walked toward the car, careful not to tread in the image which shuddered and vanished as his foot passed over it.

They drove past trees that were bare except for the tatters of leaves. There was no wind but everywhere were the signs of a gale having recently passed through, branches hanging like burnt wood. He watched a black pattern of branches scribble itself over the windshield. Light and dark brushed his face as they turned onto the highway. Cars, garage signs.

—What time is it?

—Midday exactly. How you feeling, Bud?

—Good, man.

—Don't worry about a thing, Bud.

He watched out of the side window as the car passed a cemetery, a woman walking along a narrow path between gravestones, red flowers clutched tight against the black of her coat.

—You seen Buttercup?

—She's waiting for you, Bud.

—And the boy?

—Looking real cute. He looks like you, Bud.

—Yeah?

The look in Bud's eyes: the universe smiling before there was any life in it. As far back as that. The car moving along the daylight highway. Nervous, hoping. Tonight he would sleep in the same bed as Buttercup, his wife.

.

—Bud

.

—Bud

.

—Oh, Bud, my sweet man.

Holding him in her arms. Seeing the happiness in his eyes, sobbing now he is back because she cannot think how she endured the months without him. Hearing him say,

—Hey, Butter, baby, baby.

—Bud.

Knowing that this is what it means to be with a man, to give yourself to him, this simple act of saying each other's names. Her fingers moved to the scars on his head: the lover's instinct to reach for the place of greatest tenderness.

Sniffing and smiling, her head on the pillow, she says,

—My ear is full of tears.

.

In Paris you played to half-empty houses, sometimes playing as if you were not even there. And even when you could play you moved like a sportsman who has injured his back and is never quite able to move with the same reflex energy as he did before, always aware of the effort you were making to get your fingers to the keys, knowing that too much concentration was taken up with technique, not enough left for whatever it is that makes jazz happen.

Or maybe not. I've always believed that an artist is someone who turns everything that happens to him to advantage. Was that true for you, Bud? Were you able to turn even the events of your life to advantage? The early work is what counts, everyone agrees on that. But the days you couldn't play—wasn't there something special about those performances as you struggled to learn again the language you had helped invent? Is it possible that the music was heightened by your inability to play it?—like damage to a painting enhancing a perfection that is no longer there.

·

You liked Paris, liked the smell of shops, the smell of coffee and fragrant cigarettes, the way women appeared in the spring wearing crocus dresses. Liked sitting in a café while the waiter piled up chairs and swept up checks, feeling, as you never could in New York, that you were the last person in the city to leave for home.

On afternoons when dusk drizzled perpetually over the Seine you walked by the river, exchanging nods with thin and sockless Africans. Drifted around under vast marble skies, sat outside cafés and watched the traffic swathe by, taking nothing in. Anyone who recognized you was touched for a glass of red wine which you attempted to sip slowly, smiling contentedly until the alcohol began to ferment and bubble in your head. You tried not to drink but there was always someone happy to pay the price of a drink to sit and ask questions, looking in your eyes for hidden scars, noticing the jacket misbuttoned, smelling the blood-breath of TB as you spoke.

—That's the Eiffel Tower, ain't it?

—Pardon, Monsieur Powell?

—The Eiffel Tower. You see it in pictures sometimes.

—*Oui*, Monsieur Powell.

·

Sitting on a wire chair by the side of a pond, you felt as if you were looking out over the edge of the world. Spots of rain pimpled your reflection. Two children in red bobble hats were standing nearby, one saying,

—*La flaque d'eau, l'étang, le lac, l'océan.*

—*T'as oublié la mer*, said the other. You looked at them, lost in the vastness of words.

·

Every jazz musician in Paris had showed up at the Club St. Germain: Milt Jackson, Percy Heath, Kenny Clarke, Miles, Don Byas. You arrived with Buttercup, holding yourself erect, your arm threaded through hers. You walked in like a man descending a staircase in the dark, testing each step with your foot. Your eyes showed nothing, only a little cautious happiness.

Everyone in the club watched the group of Americans gathered around the bar, hugging each other, slapping hands, pummeling affection into one another's backs, laughing, the club filling up with the curling smoke of Negro speech. Squeezing past on their way to the rest room, they smiled and said excuse me with great courtesy, were happy to stand and accept compliments, to shake and kiss hands and ask the names of those paying them such attention—before excusing themselves and rejoining the huddle at the bar. Boys whispered to their girlfriends, pointed out who was who, which one was Miles Davis. Young men sitting alone with half-empty drinks and half-read books gazed in their direction, seeking clues in everything they did, for even the way these men laughed and talked seemed touched with greatness.

Then silence thickened in the group as they looked toward the stage, the silence gaining momentum and spreading across the club. One of them whispered,

—Bud is going to play.

No one had seen you leave the group or noticed you heading for the piano until you were about to sit down on the stool. The silence grew damp. Voices in the audience:

—He can't play anymore, he can't play.

And always the murmured syllables hanging in the air:

Bud Powell Bud Powell.

The chime of ice and glass melted to nothing. Smoke writhed through pillars of light. The cash register crashed open like an alarm.

Touched the keys a few times, squared yourself and plunged into "Nice Work," not pausing to think your way through what you were going to play, everything happening instantly. Your fingers moved like you had played Gershwin's tune ever since you were a baby and could take it anywhere you wanted, everything coming as natural as breathing, not even having to think because your hands knew their way around the keyboard like a bird knew the sky. Everyone in the club felt the relief spreading out from the Americans, watching as if you had climbed onto a tightrope.

—Go, baby, go.

—Get it out, Bud, get it out.

Sweat beaded your forehead and you smiled as if nothing had ever gone wrong for you. A spotlight was shining into the side of your face, throwing a perfect silhouette onto the wall behind, a shadow that duplicated your every move, a lurching shape perched on your back, deriding you.

—Yeah, Bud.

—Go, Bud, go.

And then, like the tightrope walker wobbling, the first hint of uncertainty, hesitating over a note, faltering, recovering your balance then hesitating again, unsure of your way, the shadows of your arms screeching like a bird's wings behind you. Then stumbling, your hands becoming tangled up in each other, losing the momentum that might have carried you through a lapse in ideas, the song falling apart, the keyboard a maze you could never find your way out of, lost, then . . . then hitting a few notes but losing it, drowning in the tune like it was an ocean swallowing you up . . . Then then then. Then there was no point even touching the keyboard.

You stood up, pushing back the stool with your legs, your shadow rearing up above you. Devastation scarring your face, pouring sweat, pulling a white handkerchief out of a pocket, rubbing it over your face like a child over a blackboard, hoping to wipe yourself out, erase all memory of yourself. The silence in the club had gone from being a living breathing thing to the silence that is the absence of all life, the silence that hangs from trees after a terrible battle. You moved away from the stage. Hands slapping into each other, becoming applause. Buttercup moved toward you, hugged you, your arm reached around her shoulder, her fingers moved up to calm the nerve throbbing in your cheek, palpitating under her touch as you moved toward the group of Americans. And as they applauded, everyone in the audience, everyone, understood that there must surely be something terrible about a form of music that can wreak such havoc on a man. It was like watching a gymnast and taking such agility and strength for granted until there was a fraction of an error and he crashed to the floor. It was only then that you realized how ordinary the barely possible had been made to appear—and it is the crash rather than the perfect somersaults that expresses the truth, the essence of the activity; that is the memory which stays with you forever.

•

It's late, Bud, the music has come to an end, the candles have drunk themselves to nothing. It'll be light soon. I'm tired but you sit there as though there's no such thing as time. Are you tired? Are you tired of me talking at you like this?

Bud? Have you even heard what I've been saying? Was any of it like that, was any of it the way I've imagined it? Maybe it's all wrong but I tried. I wanted to hear your story, Bud, not tell it—failing that I wanted to tell it as you'd have wanted it told. I didn't have much to go on. I've seen people who played with you, people who played with people you played with. I even met someone who was in Harlem when five thousand people lined the streets for your funeral. Apart from that it was just the records and photos: they're all that's left now.

And this, Bud. And now this.

They stopped at a railroad crossing and in a few mo-
ments a train came clanging toward them. They
watched the long wall of freight thunder slowly past,
rails squealing under the weight. Duke still felt nostalgic
for the days when they'd crisscrossed America by train
in two Pullmans hired specially for the band: a cocoon
isolating them from Southern racists and Jim Crow red-
necks. No environment suited him better for working
than trains. Most of his writing was done on the move
or in a few snatched hours in hotels; the train offered
both the momentum of stimulation and sanctuary for
concentration. When his mother died he'd shut himself
off in a private section of the Pullman and written
"Reminiscing in Tempo"—all caught up in the rhythm
and motion of the train dashing through the South.
Again and again the chatter of trains and whistles found
its way into his music, especially in Louisiana, where
the firemen played blues on the engine whistle, smeary
haunted things like a woman singing in the night. The
railroad ran through his work as it ran through the
history of black Americans: they built the railroads,
worked on them, traveled on them and eventually there

he was, composing on them: that was the tradition he was heir to. In Texas once, a bunch of railroad workers had glanced through the window of a train pulled over in a siding and seen him hunched over a manuscript, sweat dripping onto the page. One of them tapped on the window, not wanting to disturb him but desperate just to say "Hi, Duke" or something, and he'd got up smiling and told them what he was working on—"Daybreak Express," a piece about the guys who built the railroad:

—Diggin and diggin and swingin a hammer for six months, and then the train goes by—swish . . . whoo-oo-oo . . .

Explaining his music to them, seeing the pride well up in their eyes.

All the time he'd been traveling by train he'd stored up memories like that, searching later for a tone that corresponded to things he'd seen: colors like the baked red of evening in Santa Fe or flames licking yellow in the Ohio night, the whole sky flooded with the rust-color heat of furnaces . . .

The noise of wheels and rails rang in their ears as they waited for the endless train to pass.

—Long train, said Harry at last, pushing the car into gear and clanking across the tracks.

—Sure was, said Duke as they accelerated away, looking back at the slow train hooting its way South.

Europe was less a continent than a rail network he treated as if it were a huge subway, ferrying him from one part of town, one club, to another. He traveled in suits which after a few days were crumpled as pajamas; likewise the ties which started off hugging his collar and ended up dangling around his neck like a streamer from a Christmas party. He talked to anybody: schoolkids who wanted to laugh and play jokes, drunks in the restaurant car, old women who were suspicious about sharing a carriage with a Negro until they caught the baby look in his eyes that made them think of their own sons who had grown into men without stopping being boys. Occasionally people recognized him, bought him a drink when the trolley came by; if asked he'd take out the tenor and play. Twenty years on, people would tell how they'd been on their way to Paris, had sat opposite this big, drunk black man, trilby nestling on the back of his head, shirt buttons about to bust open, egg stains down the lapel of his jacket . . . How they had spoken for a while, the American grunting out bellicose *ouis* and *non*s, laughing just at the sound of himself speaking French.

And when jazz was mentioned suddenly realizing who it was, shaking hands, feeling the soft lightish palm, gentle as you hope a bear's paw might be. Telling him how much his music meant to you, how you'd got records he made with Duke, especially "Cottontail," how Duke had once played two hundred miles from your hometown and you'd driven there and back the same evening just to see him. Asking questions about musicians he'd known and listening to his stories like a child unwrapping Christmas gifts, buying drinks every time the trolley came around and finally, certain he'd agree but still feeling awkward, asking him to play. Watching him heave the saxophone case down from the luggage rack like he was going to show you photos of his loved ones—which is exactly what he was doing—flicking open the clasps and assembling the horn, wetting the reed and fixing the mouthpiece. Clearing his throat, propping the cigarette in the ashtray and starting to play as the sunlight strobed in through a distant line of trees. Tapping his foot slowly over the clack of rails, slowing his playing down until the horn sounded so breathy it seemed a thing of flesh and blood, not made of metal at all. Now the sun was slanting in across golden fields and the way the light caught his face made you think of photos of a planet in space, the sun cresting one side and leaving the other perfectly dark. His playing gaining in intensity the slower it became, fading into a butterfly vibrato and then enveloping the carriage again with big sobs of sound. How you decided then and there, watching the flutter of his cheeks and the famous twitching tilt of the head as he drew breath, that if you ever heard anyone saying anything against Negroes, whatever the circumstances, you'd never let it pass, from now on you'd either knock them down or at the very least leave the room. How no one, not even a king or prince who hired Mozart or Beethoven to play in his salon, no one had had an experience of music as privileged or intimate as this—Ben Webster playing just for you. But more than anything how when he finished playing, when he had tipped up the horn and let the saliva drain to the floor, when the train began slowing as your station heaved into view—too soon and yet at exactly the right time because by now Ben was so drunk it could have spoiled the perfection of everything—how when you thanked him, your heart full of the pride you feel at moments of complete sincerity, how when you shook his hand and looked at him, there were tears welling up in his eyes too, leaving snail tracks down his cheeks. And then waving to him again as the train pulled out, seeing him sitting there, this big drunk man, wearing a suit that served as napkin, handkerchief, and tablecloth, waving back.

■

Yes, he was never happier than when crossing Europe by train, watching the country turn into city and back again, folks getting on and off at stations, the slam-slam-slam of doors and those first moments of almost unnoticed motion when the train pulled out again, the finger-click of heavy wheels and rails sliding together, all that weight being tugged into motion, the inertia overcome. On a train he didn't care what happened, even when he peered into the scrawled chaos of his diary and saw that as far as he could make out he was already two hours late for a gig in Naples, which was still four hundred miles away. The great thing about a train was that once you got on, it was plain sailing, took you where you wanted to go without any thought on your part—but getting on it, that was something else. Sometimes catching a train was harder than trying to catch a bumblebee. A hundred things could happen between finding out the time of the train and arriving at the station by that time. Even when you got there with half an hour to spare and decided to kill time in the station bar you could still miss the train. Like today, he'd missed the earlier train—he'd missed three earlier trains in fact. Missing trains, shit, if he had a dollar for every train he missed he'd have been a rich man; if he had a dollar for all the people he missed he'd have been a millionaire. Naples, what a motherfucker to get to.

He unscrewed his bottle, took an extra-large swig, and gazed through his reflection out into the starless European night. For long intervals there were just fields, a sudden increase in volume the only indication of when the train hurtled through a cutting. Then the face in the window was traversed by a road running parallel to the track, the balls of his eyes gazing over the scene like two pale moons. For a while the train chased the meteor lights of a car before the rails curved to the right, pulling the train reluctantly away.

He stretched out on the seat, looked up at the sagging net of the luggage rack. The carriage was filled with a barroom haze of smoke, the windows drenched with condensation. Bits of melodies came into his head and faded again like yellow lights in the windows of dark farmhouses. He pulled the trilby over his eyes and hurtled slowly to sleep.

Mouth dry as wool, he woke up from time to time to find the train paused at inexplicable places—stations with no name where no one got on or off and railway officials stood holding cups of coffee, waiting for the train to pull out before tossing the dregs to the platform.

.

He carried his loneliness around with him like an instrument case. It never left his side. After gigs, after talking to fans and maybe a few friends who happened to be passing by, after taking in a bar and staying till there was no one else to leave, after rolling back to his room, after searching for his keys and hearing them scrape around the quiet lock, after opening the door into the apartment that was always exactly as he left it, after tossing the sax case onto the sofa—after all of this, however late it was, he always came to the moment when he wanted to continue talking, to hear the clink and bubble of someone making coffee or fixing a drink. Getting back to the apartment like this, he unscrewed a bottle, took a few slugs, and sat in his shorts and vest, playing his horn as quietly as he could. While living in Amsterdam he'd phoned up friends in America at all hours of the night but now there was only the horn and with it he'd try to speak to Duke or Bean or someone else, alternating for an hour or more between the bottle and the horn.

In the morning he woke to find himself sprawled out on the sofa, cradling the horn in his arms, not seeking comfort from it so much as offering it this simple gesture of protection. Nearby a bottle lay on its side like it had had too much and keeled over, a small stain on the carpet by the neck where it had thrown up in the night. Sometimes the bottle still held a small puddle of booze but today it contained only the daylight that angled in through the windows and filled it like a ship. Still lying on the sofa, he looked around the apartment, full of the quiet that comes only at midday when everyone has left for work and the only noise is the lonesome bark of a dog, a child laughing, or the sound of workmen a couple of streets away. He ran a bath and lay smoking in the narrow tub, letting the steam moisten the parched sponge of his head. The only sound was the dripping of the tap and the splash of his movements, the squeak of his flesh on the tub. How empty your head got to be, living abroad. Still smoking, he wrapped a huge towel around himself and opened the window, letting in the cold blond sunlight. He put some waking-up music on the record player and padded over to the stove to make coffee, the pot still compacted hard with yesterday's grinds. When you had all this time there was nothing to notice but your own gestures: a hand reaching for a match or turning down the gas, waiting for water to boil.

Slicing bread, buttering toast, the crumbs falling onto his vest and shorts, listening to the first records of the day. He swallowed coffee like beer, one gulp after another, rolling the moist toast around his mouth, feeling it break up into the dark ooze of coffee.

Later in the morning—other people's afternoon was his morning—he put on his brown overcoat and hat and took a walk, wandering around the park, looking at the fallen leaves and the benches that also had their seasons. The autumn light was yellow-white, coming in so low that it glanced off anything, even dull leaves or the clipped remains of rose bushes. Someone had left a newspaper on a bench and he sat down to read it. His Danish wasn't good enough to make out many of the words but there was something satisfying about seeing the blocks and patterns of type, holding it in his hands and guessing what a given story might be about. Looking at the paper like this was a habit he'd got into since living abroad and it always made him think of the picture Fump Hinton had taken of him, Pee Wee, and Red at a TV studio back in the fifties.

Shit, Fump was always whipping out that camera—seemed to spend as much time taking pictures as he did playing bass. Didn't feel like someone taking a picture the way it normally did, though; a lot of photographers made you feel like they were sneaking something from you. With Fump it felt the way it did when a friend took money from you when he was broke but too proud to borrow and you had to talk him into accepting, telling him to think of it not as a gift but a loan, just to make him feel OK about it, like it really meant something to him.

The four of them were waiting to rehearse a short set for a TV show but there's something about men waiting in a room together, makes even a TV studio seem like a welfare office or a waiting room at a doctor's office. Pee Wee didn't look like a jazz musician at all, more like an English comic actor from the forties, the kind who play small-time officials with nagging wives. In fact he'd shot a man once, lived on nothing but scotch and brandy milk shakes for ten years, never eating—even a forkful of steak was too much for him. He needed half a pint of whiskey before he could get out of bed, got so weak he had to hug each lamppost he came to like a long-lost friend on his way to the liquor store. After that he was in the hospital for a year—liver and pancreas in tatters—and when he got out he started drinking again. He was as tall as Ben, as skinny as Ben was big.

Ben was reading the paper, Pee Wee smoking and making halfhearted attempts to make it appear his sports coat fit him: somehow it was both too big and too small at the same time. His tie grabbed him around the neck like a drunk assaulting him. Lard-white skin showed between cuffs and socks, hairless as though worn smooth by the friction of forty years of trousers. Hinton began fiddling around with his camera and then got up and clicked off a few pictures. The other three took no notice. Red reached over and took a cigarette from Pee Wee. After that Red seemed to do nothing but hitch up his trousers and say "Well . . ." or "Goddam," tilting his torso slightly forward as he did so.

Ben looked through the paper, clearing his throat. He liked to take his time sort of not reading the paper, not flicking through it, just giving it a general look-over. Red peered over his shoulder, Pee Wee rocked his foot slightly, crossed and uncrossed his legs, tried to look at anything but the newspaper which he'd bought and read earlier—but when three people are sitting in a row, one of them reading, there is nothing for the others to do except watch and wait for him to finish so one of them can pick it up and make the others wish they were holding it. Ben coughed, cleared his throat, blew his nose. Pee Wee sighed, looked at his watch, and made a sucking noise with his teeth. Red tilted again and said damn, farted. Pee Wee blew his nose like a man with pneumonia.

—Man, they ought to come out and do a trio date with the three of us here, all the noise we're making, said Ben, puffing out his cheeks, exhaling, and shuffling the paper shut.

Pee Wee crossed and uncrossed his legs, Red hitched up his trousers—by now they were close to his knees. Tilting his porkpie further back on his head, Ben gave the order they'd all been waiting for:

—Less see if we can get a drink someplace.

That was years and thousands of miles ago but even now it made him smile to think back on it. He put the paper down and watched the ballad smoke of his breath drift away, blew his nose and looked around at the nothing-moving sky, the gentle sound of raking leaves. The sky was marbled and heading toward winter, the ground hardening. The summers were so short now, everywhere he looked it was fall or winter. He saw a cyclist pedaling toward him, calling out,

—Good morning, Mr. Webster. He waved back, unsure of whom he was addressing, listening to the slow whir of the receding wheels. Everyone recognized him and treated him with the greatest courtesy. Even something as simple as that, someone smiling and calling out his name or a dog running up to be patted, was enough to make tears course down his cheeks. He'd always cried easily, as soon as he realized he'd done something wrong or as soon as anyone did something good to him, any form of sincerity made him cry.

Smashing someone to a pulp one minute, weeping the next.

.

Maybe all exiles are drawn to the sea, the ocean. There is an inherent music in the working sounds of docks and harbors and there were times when he thought that all the melancholy beauty of the blues was present in a foghorn, wailing out to sea, warning men of the dangers that awaited them.

Increasingly he liked to play close to the water; in Copenhagen, after the clubs had shut, he would walk down to the port and play there as the pale sun broke over the gray sea. The sea was the perfect audience, the perfect ear for his playing: making every note a little deeper, holding it a little longer. In the ocean light of morning or the drifting fog of early evening sailors leaning on the rails of anchored ships and dockers pausing in their unloading heard him coax a harbor tone from his horn. Sometimes a drunk sailor with a whore on one arm and tattoos on the other would lurch past and listen for a few minutes before throwing coins into the hat that wasn't there. His playing was strong and peaceful as the tides, calling out as if the land were really no more than a huge ship, drifting through the waves, heading for home. Water lapped against the quay and kept the slow time he needed, thick ropes grew taut with strain. Calling gulls wheeled and swung to the slow pendulum of his playing. Once two whales breached just beyond the shadow line and listened to the tidal cry of the blues before fluking back beneath the waves, carrying his sound with them into the depths of the ocean. When someone told him about that he cried, feeling the obscure affinity of one endangered species for another.

In Amsterdam he played by the leafy water of dark canals. In England he walked over Chelsea Bridge toward the Embankment, the lights of the bridge imparting a kindness to the crowds of people flowing toward him, the businessmen in pinstripes and brollies, the women tied up in scarves and heels. He looked down at the Thames, a river so old and tired it hardly moved, bridges stretching away in either direction until the river twisted out of sight. It was the evening rush hour, everyone crowding into pubs or hurrying home to the toast-colored lights of houses glowing through leafless trees. The evening swam in a blue haze, streetlamps pearled the navy water. Funny, the view made him homesick but the place he felt homesick for was London. Something about the ink-blue sky, the light showing through the trees, and the long slow yawn of the Thames passing beneath it all—even as you looked it felt like a memory, like something from the past you were telling folks about.

Maybe it was because London was exactly how you thought it was going to be: taxis, red buses, Buckingham Palace, pubs, and drizzle. That and the way wherever you went you seemed to find yourself in front of one of the famous tourist spots: Trafalgar Square, the Houses of Parliament, Piccadilly Circus, and Big Ben—they took a photo of him there and used it on an album cover, grinning at the pun.

He coughed and blew his nose—that was something else about London, you had colds constantly. Shit, he'd never been in such a damp place. Leaving the bridge behind him, he wandered the white streets until he came to a small pub, the sign creaking in the breeze. He elbowed his way through the cigarette smoke, ordered a beer, and made room for himself at the bar. Guys kept arriving, thrusting pound notes over his shoulder and picking up dripping pints of warm, dark beer, buying five or six at a time. The whole place was full of the uproar of men drinking, telling stories about fighting, picking up glasses as soon as they were two-thirds empty, and ordering another round. Fighting and drinking—he'd never known a place like it. Wandering around Soho during intermission on Fridays and Saturdays, he'd lose track of the number of fist-fights going on. His kind of town all right, home from home. These days he didn't fight so much himself; not long ago he'd been on the brink of wading into somebody and had restrained himself with the thought that he had to save all that fire for the horn. He still felt the familiar tugs of belligerence after the first few glasses of booze but after another five or six that passed and all the aggression was swilled out of him, pissed away, leaving him in a swamp-glow of alcohol. Getting drunk these days no longer required his active participation; it was just the state the day tended toward. Someone had once told him that glass wasn't a complete solid, and if you left a pane standing it would spread out, very slightly, at the bottom, be marginally wider there than at the top. The whole world was getting to be like that, everything spreading and oozing out, slumping to the floor. Not like the old days when the more he drank the madder he got, always finding himself in the middle of a storm of glass, breaking tables, and broken heads, picking up someone like a weight lifter and heaving him through a window. Or that time he was talking to a young white guy when a drunk sailor came and started something that Ben finished in no time at all, stomping him into the floor and going back to his drink, continuing the story he was in the middle of telling, leaning at the bar, one foot resting on the unconscious sailor's back. He was perfectly adapted to brawling; as long as no one pulled a knife he seemed impervious to the effect of blows, his body soaked it all up so that the aftereffects of a fight were indistinguishable from those of booze—except for the time he'd swung at Joe Louis and ended up with a pair of cracked ribs, so loaded at the time he didn't even feel it.

.

He had always been heavily, powerfully built and by his mid-thirties you could sense his body waiting for the chance to bulk itself out even more. As time went by, his body and his tone became almost identical to one another: big, heavy, round. Looking at him onstage now you noticed the round gut, the potbelly bags beneath his eyes in the round face—no sharp angles anywhere. When he played his eyes rolled up into his head, neck and cheeks puffed out as though he was about to become perfectly spherical. He had always liked playing slow and now his movements had slowed down to the extent that there was a definite harmony between how his body wanted to move and the sound he produced. He played ballads so slow you could hear time weighing heavily on him. In a way the slower he played the better: he'd had a long life and there was a lot he needed to put into every note. And at the same time part of him had never grown up, he had the emotions of a little boy and sometimes it was like he was just sobbing into the horn, so that even when he played something simple and pretty it could tear your heart out. He had a huge sound and hearing him coax it into such softness was like seeing a farm laborer holding a newborn animal gently in his hands, or like a man who's been working construction handing flowers to the woman he loves. On "Cottontail" he's got a sound like a prizefighter's fist but he plays a ballad like it's a creature so fragile, so cold and close to death that only the heat of your breath can bring it back to life, so weak that even your breath feels like a gale.

■

—When somebody asked about his philosophy of music Duke said, "I like great big ole tears," and Ben was like that too. He loved ballads, sentimental tunes. Somebody called sentiment unearned emotion but that doesn't apply to jazz. The emotion is automatically earned because it's so hard to make the horn sound as gentle as that, to keep swinging and make it pull tears from your heart. If you're playing jazz you're automatically earning the emotion, paying for it; the history of the music has seen to that. When Ben plays the blues or "In a Sentimental Mood" you realize how irrelevant that whole notion of sentiment is. He was never cloying because however soft he played the growl was always lurking somewhere.

■

The feeling in his ballads came from nostalgia, he was always harking back to the days of those jam sessions in Kansas City, playing all night long with everybody outblowing everybody else, surrounded by applause and friends. These days when crowds clapped at the end of a solo he reached out his right hand and waved, greeting the audience as if an old friend had just stepped into the club, sax case strapped around his shoulder, hoping to sit in. When friends did come by he found himself beaming and laughing like a slice of melon and it was only then that he realized how rarely he laughed like that, how seldom he got the chance. Not like the days spent traveling with Duke or jamming up in Harlem—like the time he'd dashed into Minton's out of the pouring rain and seen this kid playing tenor, making it wail and wriggle around like the horn was a bird whose neck he was trying to wring. Breathing heavy, dripping rain on the floor, he listened to the loops and knots of sound tying and untying themselves. Hearing the horn squealing and wailing that way was like seeing a child he loved getting hit. He'd never seen the guy before, so he just rolled up to the stage, waited for the guy to end his solo, and said, as if it was *his* horn the guy'd been messing with:

—Tenor ain't supposed to sound that fast.

Grabbed it out of the guy's hands and laid it gentle on a table.

—What's your name?

—Charlie Parker.

—Well, Charlie, you gonna make cats crazy blowing the horn that way.

Then laughed that big snorting laugh, like someone blowing their nose hilariously, and walked out into the rain again, a sheriff who had just taken a dangerous weapon off a drunk cowboy.

He wasn't backward-looking but he knew how the life of the music depended on scenes like that. Jazz wasn't difficult for him the way it became for people later on; he was always rooted in that time when people got together just to blow. The idea was to make a contribution to the music, offer it something, find your own sound on the horn or the piano or whatever it was. Guys coming along later felt they were responsible for the future of the music—not just the future of their instrument but of the music as a whole. They felt that they had to do something that was going to change it for the next ten years—until someone else came along six months later and changed it again. Agony in every note they played, doing anything to the horn just to make it sound new, strangling it till it screeched and screamed and the music got so complicated you had to study in school for three or four years before you could hope to play anything. Jazz wasn't difficult like that for him, it wasn't something you had to wrestle with and remake in your own image, jazz was just playing his horn.

■

—If you love jazz you have to love Ben. You could like jazz and not like Ornette, maybe not like Duke even, but it's impossible to love jazz and not love Ben.

■

He carried his loneliness around with him but also he carried his sound around with him as a kind of consolation. The horn was his home, the horn and the hats he didn't so much wear as live in, the porkpies and trilbies tilted so far back on his head that they clung there like skullcaps. Waking up in the morning and feeling glad that the uncrushable hat was still on his head—that was the nearest he got now to the warm sensation of being away a long time and suddenly re-

alizing you were back in your own bed. Hat and horn:
the tradition—the home he'd never have to leave.

•

—Ben said he wanted to see the English countryside,
so we picked him up from the flat where he was staying
and drove through the endless suburbs toward the
country, never quite leaving the city. Ben was struck
by how little there was to see: no railroads, hoardings,
or billboards, just a gradual thinning out of everything.
We drove past pubs which all seemed to be called the
Crown or the Fox and Hounds. Every car we passed
was black. The sky was overcast and by the time we
finally emerged into the gray countryside a light rain
had begun to fall. Clouds hugged the low hills that
rose and fell around us.

We pulled off the main road and parked, sitting for
a few moments in the engineless silence. I'd lent Ben
a pair of Wellingtons and once he had struggled into
them we trudged along a narrow lane, stomping
through puddles as we went. We passed a broken gate
and hedges growing wild with brambles, the rain so
light it was little more than a dampness in the air. We
were walking in single file, my wife in the lead and
then Ben, breathing heavily, the smoke from his cigarette smudging the air. We followed the path into a
small forest, our eyes adjusting to the captive darkness
of the trees. It rained heavily for a little while, we could
hear it drumming on the leaves high overhead. When
we got to the edge of the forest Ben said he was tired
and would wait there while we walked on. The path
took us on a long loop around the edge of fields before
trailing up a hill. Slightly concerned that Ben might
be becoming impatient, we made our way back
through the forest. Finding our way through the trees
proved difficult and within ten minutes we were com-

pletely lost—it was just luck that we stumbled on Ben exactly where we had left him. We were making our way toward the edge of the forest, thinking to retrace our steps along the path when I saw him. He looked massive, his topcoat pulled around him, porkpie hat perched on his head, utterly incongruous. I was on the point of calling out his name but there was a happiness about the scene that I didn't want to disturb. The sun was breaking through the clouds over the horizon, silhouetting some trees and dyeing others in gold light. The forest was full of the damp silence of old rain dripping through the leaves. Birds were leaving the high trees and heading across the fields. Ben was at the edge of the forest, leaning against the gatepost, looking out over the fields at the smoke drifting from a farmhouse in the distance, the clouds moving slowly over the dark hills. We stayed very still, not making a sound, as if we had suddenly come across some beautiful bird that no one had ever seen in such a place.

You ask me what his music means to me. I can't hear his music without thinking of that afternoon. To me that is what his music sounds like, that is what it means to me. That's all I can say.

It was not yet light but the darkness of night had given way to the predawn grayness when lights appear in houses and trees wait like thin cattle on the horizon.

Duke reached forward and switched on the radio, tuning in to a program looking back to the early days of jazz. They played a record by King Oliver and then picked up the familiar story of how when the whore-houses in New Orleans were closed down musicians moved up the Mississippi and jazz spread through America. Duke was hardly listening, an idea was forming in his mind. He flipped off the radio and pondered, tapping a pencil against the dashboard. Yes, maybe that's how he would do it: he'd start with someone, years from now, tuning in to a radio as he drove across the country, hearing bits of music from the past, not from Armstrong and people like that but modern guys, guys who had been around recently or were still around now but who would be dead by the time this fellow was listening— someone who hadn't lived the life, who only knew the music through records. Looking ahead to someone look-ing back: the way the music might sound thirty or forty years from now. That way he could try and get across both what the guy heard and what he was thinking as he listened . . .

—You know, Harry, I think I might have got it.

—What's that, Duke?

—Just something, he said, searching the dashboard for a piece of paper.

The sun was peering over the horizon, squinting through the black lashes of trees. As the sky turned golden blue the car imperceptibly increased its speed as if late for a rendezvous with the coming day.

America was a gale blowing constantly in his face. By America he meant White America and by White America he meant anything about America he didn't like. The wind hit him harder than it did small men; they thought America was a breeze but he heard it rage, even when branches were still and the American flag hung down the side of buildings like a star-spangled scarf—even then he could hear it rage. His response was to rant back, to rush at it with all the intensity that he felt it rushing at him, two juggernauts hurtling toward each other on a road the size of a continent.

As he cycled through Greenwich Village, the bike threatening to buckle under his bulk, the wind lay in wait at each street corner like a mob hurling filth in his face—newspapers, tins, food wrappers, grit, an oil-rag cardigan. He conducted long-running debates with other road users as he went, keeping up a steady four-block exchange of abuse with the driver of a station wagon whose wing mirror he'd inadvertently rammed with his shoulder. He yelled at anyone who got in his way—and everyone got in his way: men in trucks, cars and cabs, pedestrians, women on bikes—it made no difference, nothing made any difference. Not only people but potholes, parked cars, lights that stayed red too long.

■

His rage never left him. Even when he was calm the pilot light of his anger was blinking away, ready to erupt at any moment. Even when he was quiet some part of his head was yelling. He didn't know why he was the way he was but he knew he had to be that way and no other. His rage was a form of energy, part of the fire sweeping through him. That's why he got bigger, to try to accommodate everything going on inside him—except he would have had to be the size of a building to contain himself. He was like a country where the temperature changes vehemently every few seconds—except whatever it does it's boiling: boiling cold, boiling hot, boiling rain, boiling ice.

■

His body had its own weather, changing shape in the course of months, gaining fifty pounds in no time and then losing it again just as quickly. Sometimes he was fat, sometimes just bulky, but mostly he was getting bigger, his body assuming the shape of an old sweater.

He tried diets and pills but routinely inhaled three or four dinners an evening, each one piled high with side orders and extras, the whole thing rounded off with a couple of bowls of ice cream. He could never get enough ice cream—what flavor it was, what key it was in, didn't matter. He lost forty pounds on a diet once and no one noticed any difference, like taking a couple of slim volumes from a library the size of a house. As surely as you had to find your own sound so you had to find your own size, and tradition decreed the bigger, the better. His weight never made him sluggish; the fatter he got, the more intense he became, a holdall crammed to bursting.

People said he was larger than life—as if life was a tiny feeble thing, a jacket several sizes too small, about to rip every time he moved.

Mingus Mingus Mingus—not a name but a verb, even thought was a form of action, of internalized momentum.

Gradually he assumed the weight and dimensions of his instrument. He got so heavy that the bass was something he just slung over his shoulder like a duffel bag, hardly noticing the weight. The bigger he got, the smaller the bass became. He could bully it into doing what he wanted. Some people played the bass like sculptors, carving notes out of an unwieldy piece of stone; Mingus played it like he was wrestling, getting in close, working inside, grabbing at the neck, and plucking strings like guts. His fingers were strong as pliers. People claimed to have seen him hold a brick between thumb and forefinger and leave two small dimples where he'd pinched it. Then he'd touch the strings as softly as a bee landing on the pink petals of an African flower growing some place no one had ever been. When he bowed it he made the bass sound like the humming of a thousand-strong congregation in church.

Mingus fingus.

.

Music was just part of the ever-expanding project of being Mingus. Every gesture and word of the day, no matter how trivial, was as saturated with himself as every other: from lacing his shoes to composing "Med- itations." The whole of the man and his music is present in the briefest glimpse of him—like Hinton's photo of him reading . . .

Mingus sat down. Sitting on a chair was like subjecting it to unnecessary force but everything about Mingus was excessive. He picked up *The New York Times* and unfolded it roughly, flattened it out in the what-is-this-shit? way he always reserved for newspapers. He read with impatience, clutching it firmly with both hands as if he were grabbing it by the lapels, picking out a few lines here and there, then jumping forward and backward, pausing over some bits and then skimming whole paragraphs before going back to them again, so that he read a given article four or five different ways without ever reading it properly. He looked like someone who had trouble reading: furrowed brow, lips apparently on the verge of shaping the words like an old man listening. The chair farted and squeaked every time he moved. Keeping his eyes on the page, he ate a doughnut, tearing it in two with one hand and putting a piece in his mouth like a snake eating a bird, chewing and swallowing, washing it down with coffee, brushing crumbs off the paper. When he'd finished reading he flung the paper to the floor as if in disgust, as if he couldn't bear to look at it for a moment longer.

Or another photo of him, this time in a restaurant wearing his banker's pinstripe, bowler hat, and dark glasses: Baron Mingus. Soon after the photo he fell sound asleep. Woke up when the food arrived and promptly began ordering around the waiters in the mock English accent he'd got from Bird:

—I say, old chap . . .

Alternating between that and:—Hey, hey, you . . . waiter.

Spotting a couple at the next table looking on disapprovingly, he seized the steak with both hands and began gromphing hanks out of it, slurping at it—mmahh, nnyagh, mmmahh—like an animal gnawing the flesh of a rat it had just killed. Ready to tear the place apart if anyone said a word to him.

■

He was sacked from Duke's band for chasing Juan Tizol across the stage with a fire ax and splitting Tizol's chair in two just as Duke was setting up "Take the A Train." Smiling, Duke asked him later why he hadn't let him know what was going to happen so he could have cued a few chords, written something into the score. Duke never fired anybody—so he asked Mingus to resign.

Nobody could put up with Mingus and Mingus refused to put up with anybody or anything. He had decided that nothing would get in his way—nothing —and as a consequence life became an obstacle course. If he had been a ship the ocean would have been in his way. By the time he realized his behavior was counterproductive it had already started to pay off in its weird way.

■

For Mingus there was no such thing as contradiction: the fact that something was done or said by him lent it an automatic integrity. Besides, his music was pledged to the abolition of all distinctions: between the composed and the improvised, the primitive and the sophisticated, the rough and the tender, the belligerent and the lyrical. That which was prearranged had to have the spontaneity of reflex; he wanted to advance the music by taking it back to its roots. The most future-oriented music would be that which dug deepest into the tradition: his music.

As a young man he'd prided himself on his knowledge of Western musical theory—until Roy Eldridge told him he didn't know shit because he didn't know any Coleman Hawkins solos, couldn't sing them. He only needed to be told it to realize he'd known it all the time. He became contemptuous of pencil composers toiling away at their desks and abandoned musical notation altogether.

.

—He didn't want anything written down because that would keep everything too stable. Instead he'd play the various parts on the piano to us, hum melodies, explain the framework of the piece and the scales they could use, go through it a couple of times—singing, humming, thumping whatever came to hand— and then leave it to us to do what we wanted.

Except what we wanted had to be exactly what he wanted.

Onstage he'd be yelling instructions, cussing out the rhythm section, calling out "Hold it, hold it" halfway through a piece because he didn't like the way it was going, explaining to the audience that Jaki Byard couldn't play shit and he was sacking him on the spot, starting the piece over again and rehiring the pianist half an hour later.

His bass marched everyone along like a bayonet in a prisoner's back. On top of that you had the torrent of instructions and the ever-present threat of physical assault. No telling how anything would turn out: Sy Johnson looked up to see Mingus throw down his bass and come over to him, shoving his mouth right up to Johnson's and spitting in his face about what a useless white motherfucker he was, thumping the piano with his fists as if he had got him on the floor and was pounding his face. Johnson's terror had turned to anger and he began belting the piano as if it was *Mingus'* face.

—That white boy can really play that thing, Mingus called out, grinning above the thunder of the piano. Haha.

■

Sometimes he'd sack half the band in one night. More often, like people who move away from the fertile soil of a volcano, worn out by worrying when it will next erupt, people just quit because they couldn't bear the flood of threats and abuse. Others stayed with him, knowing that his creativity and his rage were inseparable from each other. To make his music he had to get to a pitch of volatility where there was no difference between provocation and reaction. In life and music he responded to what happened before it even happened, always fractionally ahead of the beat. But knowing that and loving him just the same were no protection against his rage. You could devote yourself to his music, his well-being, for twenty years and then something would happen and he'd be laying into you. Not liking the way Jimmy Knepper was soloing, he walked over, belted him in the stomach, and left the stage. Knepper stuck with him until he hit him again, breaking a couple of teeth, fucking up his embouchure. When that happened he called it a day and took Mingus to court. Hearing himself described as a jazz musician, Mingus gestured to his lawyer to be quiet—exactly as if he was on the bandstand, not playing how Mingus wanted:

—Don't call me a jazz musician. To me the word "jazz" means nigger, discrimination, second-class citizenship, the whole back-of-the-bus bit.

In the witness box Knepper shook his head, missing him already.

.

He bullied his way into making himself heard on every instrument. Miles and Coltrane sought musicians whose sound would complement their own: Mingus sought musicians who offered a version of himself on different instruments. Always dissatisfied with his drummers, he had just given his percussionist a public keelhauling when he met a kid of twenty named Dannie Richmond, who had been playing drums for only a year. Mingus force-taught him to play exactly as he wanted, molding him in his image.

—Don't play that fancy shit, this is my solo, man.

Dannie stayed with him for twenty years, finding his musical identity only by subsuming it in Mingus'. The fatter Mingus got, the thinner Dannie became—as if even his metabolism adjusted itself in equilibrium with Mingus'.

.

—Playing with him, there were times when you were terrified, then there were the other times when you blew with more exhilaration than you ever felt with anyone else, feeling less like a band than a charging herd as Mingus' shouts of abuse turned into hollers of encouragement:

—Talk about it, talk about it, talk about it. His voice cracking like a whip over the backs of horses:

—Yah, yah, yah.

.

When the music reached a pitch of intensity, achieved a level of pressure even higher than that inside him, a momentum so urgent that nothing could get in its way and everyone looked like they were hanging on for grim death—that was when he hollered and whooped above the music, urging it on so that he could feel the calm of the hurricane's eye, yelling and howling like Frankenstein ecstatic and aghast at the monster he has unleashed, delighted by the thought that it is all but beyond his control. Mingus happy—nothing could beat the thrill, the rush of that. At full tilt the band felt like sprinting cheetahs, cheetahs chased by an elephant that always looked as though it might trample them underfoot.

He packed his music so full of life, so full of the noise of the city, that thirty years in the future someone listening to "Pithecanthropus Erectus" or "Hog-Calling Blues" or any of those other wild steamrolling things wouldn't be sure whether that wail and scream was a horn on the record or the red-and-white siren of a prowl car shrieking past the window. Just listening to the music would be a way of joining in with it, adding to it.

■

—He cursed and threatened us, the guys in the band, but that was nothing to the way he harangued audiences, bawling people out for talking while he was playing and going on from there to deliver half-hour-long, sprawling monologues that lambasted everyone in sight, the words coming out in a hundred-mile-an-hour *drawl*, skidding and slurring all over the place. He'd get to the end of a sentence before people realized they hadn't caught the first words and by the time they got the gist of what he was saying he'd moved on to attack something else: club owners, booking agents, record companies, critics. You name it, he felt strongly about it.

His music got close to the plantation cries of slaves and his speech approached the raw chaos of thought. Spoken stream of consciousness. His thought was the exact opposite of concentration: that implies stillness, silence, long periods of intense absorption; he preferred moving very quickly, covering a lot of ground. Thought for him was setting up a string of similarities: *it's just like, same as* . . .

Some people came partly to hear his music and partly in the hope that he'd subject them to one of his tirades. Most people sat bemused, anyone who answered him back was liable to get his teeth knocked out. A drunk repeatedly requested a song Mingus didn't feel like playing. In the end he shoved the bass in the drunk's face.

—You play it.

■

When he met Roland Kirk it was like encountering a brother from whom he had been separated at birth. Kirk was like an encyclopedia of black music: he stored all this knowledge not in his head but in his body, not as knowledge but as feeling. He had all but abolished thought and raised feeling to the level of active intelligence. He took his guidance from dreams: it was in a dream that he first saw himself playing three horns at once; it was a dream that told him to call himself Rahsaan.

Kirk was like Mingus: everything he played had in it the shout, the cry that is the beating heart of black music, a cry of sorrow, of hope, of defiance, of pain. Not only that but also a greeting, something you shouted out to friends and brothers to let them know you were on your way. However else jazz changed, that cry had to be there. Strip the modal thing away and there was swing, behind swing the blues, behind the blues that shout, the field holler of slaves.

When Kirk turned up Mingus drove the blind man around in his car, taking corners fast, bumping it over potholes, pounding on the horn, and sending up fins of spray from curbside puddles, all so that Kirk could feel the journey he couldn't see, driving with the windows down so he could hear the swish of the wet road, the occasional squeak of the wipers, the tidal honk of horns. Above all this sound (even when an attempted U-turn kept the car wedged at a right angle to the dense flow of traffic for a full three minutes) Mingus maintained a monologue of questions, opinions, and assertions, pausing only to hurl gouts of invective at other drivers and cyclists.

—You tryin a ride that thing or make it fuck you up the asshole?

Every few seconds Kirk nodded enthusiastically, reaching out to touch Mingus' arm, pounding his shoulder in agreement, laughing. In the morning Kirk sat opposite him in a diner, aghast at his capacity to put away food: in the course of their drive they had stopped off at two other restaurants and he had polished off gargantuan quantities of food and drink at each one. On arrival in the diner he had wolfed down a stack of blueberry pancakes and cream and was now wading into eggs, double bacon, sausage, and hash browns, sticking his fork into the potatoes like they were still underground and had to be uprooted.

—You dig them potatoes, man?

—Not personally, said Mingus, his mouth so crammed with food the words practically had to burrow their way out.

—Yeah, but you dig 'em, right?

—Yeah, I dig 'em.

—And the eggs too.

—Yeah, the eggs are pretty good too . . . Hey, hey, waiter, some more coffee here. You want more, man?

—Yeah, I'll take some more.

While the waiter slopped coffee into their mugs Mingus looked at Kirk's dark glasses, wondering how accurately he was sensing Mingus' spirit through his voice, the weight and noise of his movements.

—Over easy, Kirk said at last.

—Yeah.

—Good, good. You know the moon might crash into the earth any day now?

—Where you hear that?

—Can't remember for sure. Not sure I even heard it at all.

—Shit, man. Mingus laughed through a spongy mouthful of toast.

—What's an egg look like, Mingus?

—A egg?

—Yeah, tell me what an egg looks like.

—How old was you when your eyes went out?

—Two.

—You ever seen the sun?

—Yeah, must've done. I remember the sun.

—An egg looks like that, like the sun. Yellow, bright, clouds around it.

—Like the sun, eh? Ha. Nice way a putting it, man. People close their eyes, they can hear the sun, if you close your eyes enough. Sometimes on the tenor I try to get a sun sound, try to get a moon sound too. Never been in touch with the moon as much as I've been in touch with the sun, or the clouds, though.

Almost before Kirk had realized what they were, the colors had begun to fade. Some nights he dreamed he saw the branches of trees fanning against a blue haze of sky, or a dog running across open space into a landscape of houses and fields. These things he had never seen—or at least he could not remember having seen them. He never dreamed of the sea but he imagined what it was like. He had heard the sea and smelled it and from that he built up a picture of a mass of water, filling the huge craters and trenches of the planet. He felt the sound as a force heaving water to and from the shore. There was something similar in the gospel music he had heard as a child, a vast sawing and rocking passing through the congregation.

The weather also had its sounds. When it snowed, all sound was muffled, the ground creaked and groaned under your feet; on bright days everything rang clear and blue; on fall evenings there was a halo of mist around everything he heard. In the city there was the ground rumble of traffic, the constant sound of horns, yells, shouts, steam hissing from vents. Silence was a certain minimum level of sound necessary to cover up other noise.

Where Kirk's eyes were, Mingus saw the reflection of his own chewing face. He wanted music to be like the sun to a blind man, or a meal wolfed down when you were hungry, as immediate and instinctive, as necessary as that. And something else too—something Kirk had made him feel absolutely certain about. There had to be another sound that must also have been heard on the plantations, just as you heard it wherever work was done, however appalling the conditions: the sound of men laughing together.

.

He dropped off Kirk and went back to his apartment, where he was met by a scene of chaos, an open window blowing a blizzard of paper across the room. Wherever he lived he accumulated stuff the way his body accumulated weight. If he went into a store and saw something he liked he'd buy a shelf's worth of whatever it was. Eventually, when he felt himself becoming hemmed in by the mess of rainy-day junk, jotted notes, and abandoned projects, he'd file everything away, picking up armloads of paper and chucking them in a desk drawer like he was throwing fuel in a furnace, or dumping stuff into the furthest corner of a room like rubbish on the outskirts of a city.

His head was a drawer crammed with the remains of intentions and fragments of what was still to come. Long compositions were full of the debris of previous ones and more and more he was moving toward a single piece which would include everything he had ever written before. Then there was the sexual fantasia of his autobiography, less a book than a huge drawer in which he crammed hundreds of pages of notes to be sorted through, edited, and ordered at a later date, a compost heap of prose. Every couple of weeks he'd shovel on some more chapters, leaving it to ferment itself down to manageable proportions. Listening to him was like reading a book printed on melting butter, periods sliding to the middle of a sentence, words slithering into each other. That's why his book was turning into such a mess: he could never make his words stick to the page.

He believed you could say everything in music but there was still more he wanted to say. He ranted at audiences from the stage, rattled off letters—to jazz journals, the U.S. Labor Department, Malcolm X, the FBI, and Charles de Gaulle—and sent threatening notes to critics: "No one could sing my blues but me, just as no one could holler for you if I decide to punch you in the mouth. So don't come near me ever in this life." On TV he demanded that a Senate committee investigate why so many black musicians had ended up like paupers. He claimed gangsters were out to get him and warned others that gangster friends of his would kill them. He said whatever he wanted to because as far as he was concerned he had nothing to keep quiet about. People asked—quietly—who the fuck did he think he was? That was an easy one to answer: he thought he was Charles Mingus. The onliest Charles Mingus.

He fought on every front he could to extricate himself from the clutches of a holding corporation called America. He wanted to own the means of production, his production. He set up his own record label and organized a rebel alternative to the official Newport festival—driving around the town with a bullhorn, getting them to come to his festival as though he were telling them to vote Mingus vote Mingus. He wanted to own his own club; a ballroom where he could play dance music; a school for music, art, and gymnastics. Nothing was ever enough. Convinced he was being ripped off right down the line, he decided to make his records available through mail order only—and almost got prosecuted himself for ripping other people off: customers sent in checks, waited for the records that never arrived, and then wrote to ask what was going on—thereby adding to the chaos at Charles Mingus Enterprises. He wasn't cut out to be an entrepreneur: he was the kind of man who, when reaching for the phone, would knock a cup of coffee off the edge of the desk and into an open drawer, thereby ensuring not only that any documents that happened to be in the drawer were ruined but also that the first thing a caller heard was not a pleasant voice saying "Hello, can I help you?" but Mingus yelling "Shit!" While speaking on the phone he felt a compulsion to eat, so that deals were negotiated through mouthfuls of chewed food, one hand reaching regularly into a sack of chips and cramming more into his already crowded jaws, the mouthpiece filling up with sprayed crumbs and the conversation, like bad reception on a radio, often lost in static bursts of chomping. The gist of what he was saying was perfectly clear anyway; negotiating for Mingus typically amounted to yelling, "You stinking white motherfucker asshole, you better watch out 'cause I'm gonna come down there and stomp you," before shattering the phone into its cradle. Picking it up again a few seconds later and hearing a dying squawk instead of the dial purr he wanted, he flung the whole unit at a wall, grunting with temporary satisfaction.

He wrecked stuff as quickly as he accumulated it. All over New York were the remains of things he'd smashed up, their value enhanced by being half ruined. One night at the Vanguard he demanded instant payment from Max Gordon. There was no money around, so Mingus had to make do with threatening him with a knife and smashing bottles on the floor like a cop from prohibition confronted with a stash of bootlegged liquor. Looking around for something else to smash, he put his fist through a light fixture. They called it the Mingus light and left it that way, something for tourists to ask about. He was a Midas of destruction: everything he wrecked turned to legend.

.

In Germany he went on a rampage, smashing doors, microphones, recording equipment, and cameras in hotels and concert halls alike—a protest against the Nazi hospitality he claimed lay waiting for the band wherever they played. Mingus and the rest of the band went home, but Eric Dolphy stayed on to play some gigs of his own. When he died in Berlin, surrounded by people who didn't even know who he was, all of the cruelties and injustices of the music's history seemed to Mingus to have converged on sweet, gentle Eric. Jazz was a curse, a threat hanging over anyone who played it. He'd written "So Long, Eric" as a farewell and now it became a requiem.

He had needed Dolphy. His playing was so wild, so beyond anything you expected that Mingus found himself calmed by it. Mingus could play wild and free as anyone but as far as he was concerned the kids who produced the clatter and squawks of the avant-garde hadn't even bothered to learn their instruments. He'd briefly got tangled up in some acid-brained spontaneous invention project of Timothy Leary's and what he'd told Leary applied equally to all the noise merchants of the new thing, the new music.

—You can't improvise on nothin, man, he'd said, shaking his head at the shambles around him. You gotta improvise on somethin.

At best, free jazz was a diversion which might even help in the long run: after a while people would see it was a dead end and maybe then they'd realize the only true way forward was to make the music swing harder. Twenty years from now, once they'd got all the squawking out of their system, people like Shepp would go back to playing the blues, you could bet on it.

People thought Dolphy avant-garde, experimental, but Mingus heard him crying out as if trying to reach all the dead slaves. Mingus had always known that that was what the blues was: music played to the dead, calling them back, showing them the way back to the living. Now he realized part of the blues was the opposite of that: the desire to be dead yourself, a way of helping the living find the dead. His hollering now was a call to Eric, asking him the way, asking where he was. His solos got heavier, they swung with the movement of a gravedigger's shovel, weighed down by damp earth.

One time he and Bird had been talking about reincarnation in the intermission between sets.

—You got something there, Mingus. Let's talk about it on the stand, said Bird, picking up his horn and walking toward the stage. He and Eric had done the same thing: speaking to each other on the stand, alto and bass explaining, qualifying, and contradicting each other. Now he called to Eric but no voice came back. He knew Eric could hear him but he wasn't playing back. That would take time. It was like the way a son gradually comes to look like his father; it is not until after the father has died that his spirit makes itself felt in every one of the son's gestures. So it would be a while before the tradition absorbed the spirit and gestures of Dolphy so that when someone played bass clarinet or alto in a certain way it would be as though the instrument were a medium through which the dead could sing, through which Eric could speak. You could hear Bird, Hawk, and Lester Young everywhere—you would never hear Eric as pervasively as that but someone somewhere would always be calling to him and if they called out hard enough he would answer, make himself heard.

Eric Eric Eric.

And when Mingus himself died you wouldn't have to call out hard to hear him, all you'd have to do would be to pick up the bass and he'd be there in the room: you'd hear him in Dyani and Hopkins and Haden just as you heard Pettiford and Blanton talking through him.

So he named his son Eric Dolphy Mingus, not in memoriam but in anticipation.

.

At the 5-Spot he was wearing an old sweater with holes at the elbows and torn trousers, looking like a poor raggedy farmer—clothes intended to shame any dinner-jacket whites who came to hear his music. He was playing "Meditations," trying to reach out to Eric, to talk to him, but hearing instead just the ice-and-glass tinkle of the voice of a woman sitting right by the stage, talking so hard she was oblivious to where she was, let alone who was onstage or what he was playing. His temper was always a split second ahead of what he realized he was doing. By the time he was conscious of yelling at her he had already kicked her table over. By the time it hit the floor he was stalking off the stage. When the scatter of glass died down he heard her shouting something back at him. A drunk at the bar was joining in too, his voice the sound a buzzard would make if it could speak.

—Charlie, that was not nice, that was not nice at all.

For a moment he considered thumping the guy's head against the bar until it smashed like a bag of sugar, but whenever the thought occurred like that, in anticipation of the event, it meant nothing would happen—or something else would, something so sudden that it would take even him unawares. He was gripping the bass by the neck, glowering at the audience, pleading with them. He turned toward somebody who said afterward that as he glared at him like that he saw the whole of Mingus' life flashing through the bassist's eyes. For a second he knew exactly what it felt like to be Mingus: the weight of everything, the way he couldn't shrug off or hide from anything, the way he was completely at the mercy of what he was feeling.

He hit the bass against the wall: a sharp crack, a resonant echo from the strings and he was left holding the neck, still attached to the body of the bass by the four strings, so that it was like a puppet-turtle—which cracked, splintered, and parted under his weight like a varnished sea of wood as he walked straight through it. He let the neck fall from his hands, everyone silent except for the drunk calling out,

—Oh, heavy, Charlie, heavy.

Looked at the guy again without any thought of hitting him. His rage had turned pale, transparent, and desperate as water dripping in a sink. Walked out into the street, dragging the silence of the club with him.

■

In Bellevue smells were the first things he noticed: the bathroom cleanliness of everything, then the white light of tiles and walls. Then sound, the glinting noise of clean utensils, the squeak of trolley wheels moving through the long corridors of the mad and then, at night, the screaming. All through the night someone was screaming; even while he slept Mingus could hear it shrieking through his dreams, a Hellview of Bellevue. In the mornings there was the busy hospital silence again and no one mentioned the night screams which lay in wait at the end of each day. Sedated, his rage dulled by medication, calm lying over him like a blanket, he lay in bed and watched the ceiling, the lights like planets in a white sky.

■

He subdued the bass but couldn't conquer it. Sometimes he draped his arm around it like an old friend. Other times it began to seem a huge instrument and he lugged it around like a sack of rocks, almost too much for him, almost overwhelming him. If he didn't practice constantly the strings sliced his fingers when he touched them. Not only that but the stiffness in his fingers never left now, some days they felt not simply stiff but numb. His toes too. There were days when it became difficult to move his hands at all and he felt the numbness inching up his arms toward his shoulders, so gradually it was possible to convince himself that it was not progressing at all.

In Central Park a bacon streak sunset reddened the frozen ground. He watched ice squeezing the warm center of the pond and knew that he was becoming paralyzed. Like flamenco—he'd realized this years ago in Tijuana—the movement of jazz was centrifugal, you felt it like a pulse constantly escaping the body, moving from the heart outward, leaving in its wake tapping feet and clicking fingers that registered the intensity of its movement like leaves in the wind. Paralysis was the exact denial or contradiction of that movement of jazz: it started at the extremities, at the fingers and toes, and worked its way inward, working its way to the heart, obliterating all trace of its progress.

It became more difficult to find the notes on the bass—he knew where they were but was unable to make the fingers grip. More and more he resorted to the piano but soon his fingers felt too wooden for the keyboard. As it became impossible to play so it got harder to compose. He wasn't like Miles, who heard the music and then simply transferred it from his head to the instruments. Mingus didn't hear music until he was making it. Composition was just performing quietly, without an audience, but to compose he had to play and he was finding it impossible to play. Mingus' music was just Mingus, the movement of the music simply his own movement and as he began to lose

mobility so the music began to lose momentum, becoming immense and unmoving—a noun.

.

He picked up the phone, slowly, like someone lifting
a barbell to build up their biceps. It was Kirk, Rahsaan,
the first time Mingus had heard from him in over a
year. Just after they'd last spoken Kirk had had a stroke
that left one side of his body paralyzed. Doctors told
him he would never play again. At first he couldn't
even walk, then when he'd learned to walk he set about
climbing stairs and when he'd done that he'd tried to
blow the horn again. It had taken six months to get
his strength back but now he was playing again, he
told Mingus. Even though one side of his body was
still paralyzed.
   —How you playing if you're half paralyzed, man?
   —Still got one arm, don't I? Haha.
   —You play a horn with one arm?
   —Played three with two, so one with one ain't so
hard . . . Hey, you there, Mingus?
   —Yeah, I'm here, man, he said, tears pricking his
eyes.
   —I'm playing in town next week so come by.
   —I'll be there, man.

.

He watched from the bar as Kirk was helped onto
the stage festooned in his usual regalia of bells, hat,
wild clothes. Talking and grinning, recognizing folks
by the sounds of their voices. He arranged everything
and then blew, blew, blew—one arm squirreling up
and down the keys, the other hanging limp at his side,
dangling there like something irrelevant, heaving and
puffing like he was trying to keep death itself at bay.
Blind, half his body paralyzed, the body barely strong

enough to remain upright, barely strong enough to contain the energy that was pouring from him, pouring off the stage and filling the room. At the end of his solos he collapsed into a chair, breathing heavily like a boxer between rounds, head reeling from the blows he'd taken, flexing the fingers of his playing hand until he was strong enough to play again. A blind man who had risen from the dead. Watching him, Mingus felt the red ice of his blood tingle in numb hands.

•

When he couldn't control his fingers enough to play the piano he sang into a tape recorder. In the past, records he'd made had sat on studio shelves for a couple of years before being released. Now record companies were eager for everything that he came up with, just the germ of an idea would be enough. Scattered around were various fragments of compositions and at some stage in the future, like when a famous writer leaves a novel unfinished at the time of his death, someone would try to use these notes and construct entire works from them. For a long time no one had wanted his autobiography but in years to come they would be hunting down the missing pages they made him throw away. Even tapes of him speaking, mouthing off, even these would be reprocessed and released on record. In bars and clubs people would boast of how Mingus had once bawled them out, thrown them down a flight of stairs, smashed up their home. He was sure of it.

•

His reaction to winning a poll for best bassist was to wonder why he didn't get it when he was young, when he was hell on wheels. Thinking what he'd have done with the money if he'd played safe and reaped the rewards of working as a studio musician, he said he'd like a house with wheels on it. He'd been hell on wheels, he wanted a house with wheels, now he was confined to a chair with wheels.

Even talking was becoming difficult. His tongue lay in his mouth like an old man's dick. Forming words was like talking through a mouthful of wool. His body was becoming a dungeon, a prison whose walls were constantly moving inward, only his intensity to keep them at bay. Someone said Mingus' intensity killed him, but his intensity was keeping him alive too.

■

Then at the White House, an all-star concert and party—in official recognition of the great contribution jazz had made to American culture and the world. A stupid event that was also a great event. Everybody was there—not Bird or Eric or Bud—but everybody who was alive was there. He was in a wheelchair, unable to move his arms or legs, trapped inside himself. When they called for a round of applause for the greatest living composer in jazz and everyone rose at once and gave him a standing ovation he broke down, tears streaming down his face, his body convulsed with great heaving sobs—the President running up to comfort him.

■

He traveled to Mexico, hoping the sun would thaw him, unlock the pack ice that was trapping his blood. He sat in the sun, surrounded by the still heat of the desert, his face shaded by the brim of a huge sombrero. His body had become so still he could barely feel himself breathe. Nothing moving anywhere. The sun was a copper cymbal that didn't move. It hung in the same place for three days in an unchanging sky, no wind, not a grain of sand twitching.

When he was very weak he saw a bird hovering high in the sky, even its wings perfectly still. Its shadow lay in his lap; summoning all his energy he found the strength to stroke it, to ruffle its feathers.

It was daylight by the time they finally stopped for breakfast. Stiff from so many hours in the car, they walked
awkwardly into the diner, the screen door slamming
behind them. The place was already crowded and noisy
with truckers, too busy chewing to take any notice of
Ellington in his old blue sweater and crumpled trousers.
Morning sun tumbled through the windows.

Yawning, Duke ordered the meal he had been living
off for God knows how many years: steak and grapefruit,
coffee. Harry asked for eggs and watched Duke slowly
stir his coffee: there was an air of sleepiness in everything
he did but it was the sleepiness of someone who has just
woken up—never of someone about to go to sleep. The
bags under his eyes suggested a backlog of missed sleep
that would probably take ten years to clear. Instead of
paying it back, though, he found the sleep debt continuing to mount up as he scraped by, night after night, on
four or five hours. Perhaps it was their collective wear-
iness that kept the core of the band together: after a
while frazzled tiredness gets to be addictive, you depend
on it to keep going. People kept telling Duke to ease up,

to rest and relax—which was all very well, but what was he going to rest and relax at?

They ate in silence and as soon as he had finished Duke started in on his dessert: dozens of assorted vitamins washed down with water.

—Ready, Harry?

—Guess so. Let's get the check.

They both cast around for the waitress, already looking forward to getting back in the car.

He sat on the edge of the bed, playing softly, hunched over the trumpet like a scientist staring into a microscope. Naked except for a pair of shorts, one foot tapping a beat slow as a clock in an old house, the bell of the trumpet almost touching the floor. She pressed her face against his neck, wound her arms around his shoulders, ran a hand down the slow curve of his spine as if the notes he played were determined by the patterns traced on his skin by her fingers, as if he and the trumpet were a single instrument played by her hand. Her fingers climbed the notches of his spine again until she came to the splinters of razored hair at the back of his neck.

When she had first listened to his records his playing was so frail and delicate it seemed almost feminine, self-effacing to the point that his solos ended before she even noticed they had begun. It was not until they became lovers that she was able to hear what made his playing special. At first when he played like this, after they had made love and she drifted on the edge of sleep, she had thought he was playing for her. Then she realized that he never played for anyone except himself. It was listening to him like this, lying with her legs apart, feeling his come sliding coolly from her, that she understood, quite suddenly and for no reason, the source of the tenderness in his playing: he could only play with such tenderness because he'd never known real tenderness in his life. Everything he played was a guess. And lying here now, noticing the valleys and dunes formed in the creased sheets, damp with a light dew of sweat, she realized how wrong she had been to think that he played for no one but himself: he didn't even play for himself—he just played. He was the exact opposite of his friend Art, who put everything of himself into every note he played: Chet put nothing of himself into his music and that's what lent his playing its pathos. The music he played felt abandoned by him. He played the old ballads and standards with a long series of caresses that led nowhere and subsided into nothing.

That was how he had always played and always would. Every time he played a note he waved it goodbye. Sometimes he didn't even wave. Those old songs, they were used to being loved and wanted by the people who played them; musicians hugged them and made them feel brand-new, fresh. Chet left a song feeling bereft. When he played it the song needed comforting: it wasn't his playing that was packed with feeling, it was the song itself, feeling hurt. You felt each note trying to stay with him a little longer, pleading with him. The song itself cried out to anyone who would listen: please, please, please.

And hearing that you realized not just the beauty but the wisdom that was in these songs. Put them all together and they were like a book, a dream-guide to the heart: "Every Time We Say Goodbye," "I Can't Believe You're in Love with Me," "The Way You Look

Tonight," "You Go to My Head," "I Fall in Love Too Easily," "There Will Never Be Another You." It was all there, all the novels in the world wouldn't tell you more about men and women and the moments flashing like stars between them.

Other musicians searched the old songs for a phrase or melody they could elaborate and transform, or they'd use the horn to sing themselves into the song. With Chet the song did all the work; all Chet had to do was bring out the bruised tenderness that is there in all old songs.

That's why he never played the blues. Even if he played a blues it wasn't really the blues because he had no need of the fellowship, the religion, the blues implied. The blues was a promise he could never keep.

He lay the trumpet on the bed and walked to the bathroom. Hearing the door click shut, she was struck by how even this tiny departure was tinged with sadness. Every time a door closed behind him it felt like a premonition of the final separation that was to come just as every note he played in a song was a premonition of the last—as if improvising was a form of clairvoyance, as if he was playing elegies for the future.

He was a man who seemed always to be leaving. You'd arrange to meet and he'd show up three or four hours late, or not at all, or he'd disappear for days, weeks at a time and leave no number or explanation. And the surprising thing was how easy, how addictive it was to love a man like that, how you felt a sense of abandonment that was akin to companionship—so close did he bring you to the loneliness that everyone carries around in them, the loneliness you glimpse in the imploring faces of strangers on a half-empty subway. Even after they had made love and he slipped from her, even then, minutes after coming, she felt herself losing him. When some men made love to you your body bore the imprint of passion like a child growing in your womb. They could be gone for a year and still your body felt full of them, full of their love. Chet left you feeling empty, full of longing for him, full of hope that next time, next time . . . And by the time you realized he could never give you what you wanted he was the only thing you wanted. She felt tears nettling her eyes and thought back to something a friend of Chet's had once said to her about his playing, that the way he held notes made you think of that moment just before a woman cries, when her face becomes brimful of beauty as water in a glass and you would do anything in the world not to have hurt her the way you have. Her face like something so calm, so perfect, you know it can't last but that moment, more than any other, has something of the quality of eternity about it: when her eyes hold the history of everything men and women have ever said to each other. And then you say to her "Don't cry, don't cry," knowing those words, more than any others in the world, will make her weep . . .

In the bathroom he splashed silver water on his face, looking up at the mirror through the mercury drops that fell through his hands. Staring back at him was a face whose features seemed controlled by some internal gravity that pulled everything inward. Shrunken shoulders, arms marked by bruises and broken veins. He lowered his hands and watched the reflection do the same, hands sprouting like antlers from thin wrists. He smiled and the reflection leered back, a ghastly smile that showed no teeth, only hard gums.

He felt no fear at this sudden apparition. For all he knew thirty years could have passed since he first glanced at the mirror. Time happened to him like that. It was possible to hold a note on the trumpet for just long enough to make it seem like eternity. While it lasted it seemed it would never end.

·

It had happened once before, just as suddenly, as he was walking to a rehearsal studio one November afternoon a couple of years ago. Hunched against a grit-laden wind he caught a glimpse of his leather-coated reflection in the mirrored front of an office block across the street. He liked this happening, suddenly seeing himself as someone else in a long Bayeux of images. The sequence of reflections was interrupted briefly by the entrance to the offices and when he looked again he was startled to see, instead of his own reflection, an old man in a leather coat looking back at him. Drawing closer, he made out more details of the man who was shuffling toward him, returning his gaze like a threat: a face lined with tree-bark wrinkles, beard, long scrawny hair, dull eyes that peered out over an arm's-length horizon. He moved to the edge of the sidewalk and the old man did the same, staring patiently into the traffic, mouth set in that way he'd noticed before in old women in Europe, making them seem fully at home in suffering and aches: lips sealing the pain in, never letting it cry out because then they'd have to admit how hurt they were and it would be unendurable. Already sure of what would happen, he waved at the old man and watched him perform, si-multaneously, a mirror image of the gesture. Under-standing the significance of what had occurred so clearly that he did not even need to think about it, he turned into the sharp edge of the wind and walked on.

·

He walked out on his women as the whim took him, often for no reason at all. Usually he went back to them, just as—time after time—he went back to certain songs. He had left so many women he sometimes wondered if that wasn't what attracted them to him: the knowledge that he would leave them. To be completely selfish, untrustworthy, unreliable—and vulnerable—that was the most attractive combination in the world. He had told this to a woman once and she had said knowing that was the cheapest wisdom in the world, you could get it from any pimp.

The same woman said she could read Tarot cards and palms, offered to tell his future. He was twenty-eight and thought what the hell. He sat opposite her, looking at the gift-shop crystal ball and the candlelit cards spread out before him, fascinated by the colors and beauty of what they depicted: a world of images simpler and even more inclusive than that offered by the songs he sang and played.

—All the permutations and possibilities of life are contained in these images, she said seriously.

He watched her hands arranging the deck, pointing to one card and then another, listened to the long tale of woe the next twenty years held in store for him. He let her finish, saw her waiting for some reaction from him, lit a cigarette, exhaled a thin mist of smoke, and, laying a hand on her knee, said,

—So what's the rush?

■

There were always women—and there was always the camera. The record business wanted to promote a white star in an otherwise black firmament and Chet was a dream come true. He had that middle-distance look in his eyes, the cowboy thing, but he also had the poise of a shy girl peeking around her shoulder at the camera, hiding behind herself. He seduced the camera, gave himself to it. Onstage at Birdland, eyes shut, one arm hanging limp at his side, hair falling over his forehead, trumpet raised to his lips like a brandy bottle—not playing the horn but swigging from it, not even swigging from it, *sipping* it. Bare-chested, pouting in Halima's arms, trumpet resting in her lap. Bologna 1961, dressed in tuxedo and bow tie, Carol in black and pearls, men touching her bare arms as they squeezed past, the reflex flash of cameras all around, people treading on each other's toes, spilling drinks and pushing by. They stayed only a few minutes, making their way outside through the crowds of photographers and image-pushers. Walking into the cool evening, feeling the hard angles of bone in the softness of her shoulders, her hand around his waist. The cameras still there as he was handcuffed and hustled by jaw-faced police to the courtroom in Lucca. Soon the police began to relish the exposure, smiling for the cameras as they led him through security doors, grinning by his side as Chet looked out of the courtroom at the audience of photographers, flashes exploding like scattered applause as he stood there, gripping the bars with the lemme-outta-here intensity everyone expected. Still waiting when he emerged from prison the following year as if stepping through the VIP gate of Idlewild.

•

Their last conversation had been very simple:
—You owe me.
—I know.
—This is the last warning.
—I know.
After that the two of them stared at each other for several seconds, pleased at the brief poetry of this exchange. To round things off Manic ran through the scales of threat.

—I'm giving you two days. You've got two days. Two days is what you've got.

Chet nodded—two days—and the duet was over.

Chet had been buying from him for six months and Manic, pleased to have a prestige customer, had broken his own first rule: no credit—ever. Twice he'd let Chet walk away with a couple of bags on credit and both times he'd showed up with the money a few days later. From there it was a short step to Chet running up a tab which, for a while at least, he settled promptly, often throwing in an extra couple of hundred as advance payment against future purchases. That worked fine for a while and then Manic began having to remind him that the debt was getting a little out of hand—and again that nudge was enough to make sure Chet settled whatever was outstanding within a few days, a week at the most. Then it got to the point where Chet not only bought on credit but borrowed money too. Interest was mounting up, Chet's promises—tomorrow, man, tomorrow—had been going on for weeks and Chet's face had the look of water swirling down the drain. Hence their last conversation.

Manic had been feeling bad himself. As far as he could remember, he hadn't slept for a month, not a wink, snorting sulphate and gobbling amphetamines until his head felt brittle as burnt paper. It was so long since he had slept that he could feel his brain eating itself away like a starving man's stomach, trembling so much he was practically vibrating. His thoughts were turning into snatches of dreams lasting maybe a couple of seconds, full of plot, color, and action.

Chet was in the Moonstruck diner when they met again, slurping from a cup of sump-oil coffee. Manic saw him through the window, strode in, and flipped around a chair, straddling it so he could lean on the back like a beer-gut sheriff in a Western whose quiet manner is full of slumbering menace. Manic's own manner was anything but slumbering: he was thin as a pole and twitching like an insect; any menace he gave off was like a scared dog's. He ordered coffee and emptied packets of sugar into the cup until it was thick as glue. His breath stank and he made a point of keeping his face inches from Chet's, making him inhale the reek. He felt like he'd just seen every film ever made six or seven times in an afternoon and had now stepped out into the light, shocked to find the world and daylight still there. He was wondering what to do, lost in the freeze-frame intensity of his head when Chet's breakfast arrived. Manic watched him sprinkle the plate with salt and said,

—How come you never smile, Chet?

—I guess I just lost the knack.

—I gave you two days.

Chet was staring into the dead pool of coffee, ceiling lights glinting in it like a glimpse of bright fish. A cigarette fumed in an ashtray.

—That was eight days ago. Double twice as long, said Manic, pulling the knife from Chet's hand and jabbing it into the yolk which ran yellow over the plate.

Before coming here he'd known that however badly he wanted the money he enjoyed these rituals of threat more; if Chet played along, spoke his lines, and contributed to the cinema of the moment, he knew he'd give him more time to pay. Today, though, Chet seemed indifferent to the whole charade and this made Manic feel like a jerk.

—Have you got it?

—No.

—Are you gonna get it, motherfucker?

—I don't know.

Manic was holding the knife, Chet the fork—as if the two of them were a pair of hands. On an impulse and without anger, desperate to inject some energy into this lifeless scene, Manic flung the coffee in his face. Chet flinched, dabbed at his face with a napkin, the coffee not hot enough to scald. Manic waited— maybe next he'd jab a knife in his eye, like he did with the egg. Chet continued sitting there, his breakfast awash in a brown slop of coffee.

Manic could think of nothing to say or do. The scene had no momentum in it. Normally one move led to another but Chet was sitting there like a dead end. Glancing at the table, he picked up a ketchup bottle by the neck, drew it back behind one shoulder, and swung it hard as a baseball bat at Chet's mouth. Not because he wanted to or because the situation demanded it but because there was nothing else to do. The bottle shattered, splatting the wall with glass and a thick gloop of sauce. His mouth was full of glass and the shards of teeth, the tomato taste of blood. Amazingly he was still sitting at the table like someone patiently waiting on dessert—until Manic was laying into him again and he felt the chair capsize and he was on the floor, a succession of kicks pouring into his head and jaw. He felt the table going over on top of him, a plate bouncing off his head and onto the floor, one hand sliding in a yellow ooze of egg. He tried crawling around the table and escaping into the maze of chair legs but then these were uprooted and came avalanching down on him. On a tide of shouts and screams from the other diners a deluge of water came draining over him, more coffee, a vase of flowers, a sugar shaker gritting the floor with white crystals.

Then it was over and he was pinned in this collapsing tunnel of broken furniture, hands jabbing on jagged glass and clumps of teeth, the floor a swamp of ketchup, coffee, and vase water, three yellow tulips floating in the mess. Mustering all his strength, he surged to his feet like a man pushing off from the bottom of a pool, egg yolk, crockery, and strips of bacon dripping from him, his mouth smeared across his face. The first thing he saw was a waiter standing nearby, coffeepot in hand as if about to offer a refill; behind him the open mouths of diners, suspended in their chewing of omelettes, bagels, and pancakes. Feeling himself collapse, he stretched out a hand and daubed a wall with an atrocious palm print before careering out of the door and into the street, covered in the remains of a nightmare breakfast. Outside, San Francisco reared up and fell away in a mountain sea of streets, a yellow bus cresting huge waves, heading toward him like an ocean liner.

.

That was in '72. By '76 he looked like he'd been meant to look all the time, maybe a little worse. His face made a return to the land, he looked the way he would have if he'd never left Oklahoma: a beard, Levi's jacket, jeans, T-shirt. The kind of guy you saw all over the Midwest, leaning on a bar, talking cars and drinking Coors from the bottle, smacking his lips when a woman came through the door. Kind of guy who'd taken twenty years to end up drinking in the place where he'd had his first beer. Working in a gas station, listening to a transistor radio, surrounded all the time by the smell of gasoline, the glint and shine of cars. Watching other men's wives as he wiped the blob and splatter of insect limbs from the windshield.

.

Even when his teeth had gone and his eyes had leathered over with defeat, even then the image-dealers and lens junkies were there, astonished at the speed with which he had changed from a pale Shelley of bebop to a wizened Indian chief, relishing the obviousness of it all, the parable of the face. If they'd looked more closely they'd have seen how little the face changed, how constant his expression remained: the same look of vacant questioning, the same gestures. That was how, in spite of everything, you could go on loving him for thirty years: his features caved in, his arms shriveled like winter trees, but the way he picked up a coffee cup or a fork, the way he moved through a door or reached for a coat—like his sound, these gestures remained the same. The same gestures and the same poses: cigarette dangling from his fingers, trumpet held loose, swinging lightly from his hand. In 1952 Claxton photographed him cradling the trumpet, head bowed, hair slicked back, eyes gazing girlishly at the camera. In 1987 Weber photographed him the same way—except the eyes are just shadows; everywhere he seems to be disappearing into darkness just as the voice trails off into nothing, as the horn peters into silence. In 1986 Weber photographed him in Diane's arms, head pressed into her shoulder just as Claxton had shown Lilli clutching him to her chest thirty years previously, the same look of the baby consoled by a mother, the same sense of self-surrender.

.

The songs had their revenge: he abandoned them time and time again but always came back, always returned to them. Whereas before he had taken each song as he pleased, needing only to whisper a few phrases to make it cry out, now they felt nothing, were left untouched by his playing. Picking up the trumpet left him with no breath to blow it and more and more he sang the words of songs, his voice wispy and soft as a baby's hair. Sometimes he caressed his old songs so gently they remembered what they had once felt, how easily they had been purpled by his fingers and breath—but mainly they took pity on him, offered him shelter he barely had the strength to accept.

.

Wherever he went people wanted to know him, talk to him, say what his music had meant to them. Journalists asked him questions so long the answer required only a grunt of affirmation or denial. Of all the things that had not interested him, talking had probably interested him less than anything. He sometimes wondered if he'd ever had an interesting conversation in his life. He liked to be around talkers, though, people who didn't expect him to say anything in return. His playing was like that too, a way of saying nothing, shaping silence, lending it a certain tone. His playing was intimate because it was like someone sitting opposite you, concentrating on what was being said, waiting unhurriedly for his turn to speak.

In Europe people hung on his every note, flocking to see him because every performance was potentially his last, hearing in his music the scars of everything he'd been through. They believed they were listening closely—getting inside the music—but really they were not listening closely enough. That pain wasn't there. That's just how he happened to sound. He'd have sounded that way whatever happened to him. There was only one way he could play, a little faster a little slower, but always in the same groove: one emotion, one style, one kind of sound. The only change came from debility, from the deterioration of his technique—but that deterioration of his sound also enhanced it, imbued it with the illusion of pathos which would not have been there if his technique had survived the damage he inflicted on himself.

Those who saw in his life the tragedy of broken

promise, of wasted talent and squandered ability were also wrong. He was talented and real talent ensures it is not wasted, insists on its own capacity to flourish. Only the talentless waste their talent—but there is also a special kind of talent that promises more than it can ever fulfill: those are the terms it comes with. That's how it was with Chet, you can hear it in his playing, that's what gives it that quiet suspense. Promise—that's all there was ever going to be, even if he'd never so much as seen a needle.

■

In Amsterdam he stayed close to his hotel, taking little walks and pausing on bridges while lank gangs of junkies shuffled past, unaware of their patron saint watching from the shadows. The city whizzed around him: crossing roads, he looked each way four or five times but was constantly lurching clear of approaching trams, blaring cars, and the ringing bells of ancient bicycles. A city made of windows, hiding nothing. He walked past windows that were red with the lips of waving girls, antique shops that looked like homes, antique homes that looked like shops. He hardly spoke and when he did it seemed just a coincidence that his mouth happened to be shaping the words that hung in the air like mist. He'd heard of people kept artificially alive on a life-support system and it seemed to him that that was what his body had become—and when it was turned off he wouldn't even notice.

Back in the hotel he watched fragments of videos, dialed random numbers on the phone, smoked and waited, letting the room grow dark around him. By the window he looked out at the café lights dappling the canal like leaves, heard bells tolling over the dark water. That old story about how when you die the whole of your life flashes before your eyes. His life had been drifting before his eyes for as long as he could remember, for twenty years at least, maybe that was how long he had been dying, maybe the last twenty years were simply the long moment of his death. He wondered if there was time to get home again, to wherever it was he was born, Oklahoma, becoming a rock in the desert. Rocks were not dead, they were like land versions of fish that lie on the ocean floor passing themselves off as something else. Rocks were the state gurus and Buddhists strived to attain, meditation turned from an act to a thing. Heat ripples were the signs of the desert breathing.

In the tile glare of the bathroom he glanced at the mirror and saw no reflection at all, nothing. He positioned himself directly in front of the mirror, stared straight ahead, and saw no trace of himself, only the towels, thick and snow-white, hanging on the rail behind him. He smiled but the mirror corroborated nothing. Again he felt no fear. He thought of vampires and the undead but it seemed more like he had entered the realm of the unliving. He stared at the mirror, thinking of the hundreds of photos of him that existed on records and in magazines all over the world. From the table in the main room he fetched a record cover showing a photo Claxton had taken years ago in LA. Back in the bathroom he held it in front of him and looked at the image in the mirror. Hanging in space, framed by the towels and tiles of the bathroom, the mirror showed him sitting at the piano, face reflected in the lid, perfect as a tousle-haired Narcissus at the pond. He stared for several minutes, lowered the record, and once again there was only the snow expanse of towels.

The wet road shone silver in the midday sun. The sky was clear except for a pale smudge of moon. For the last stretch of the journey Harry had been nursing the nagging feeling that the car hadn't been running so good. When he looked at the fuel gauge he was surprised to find it already hovering toward Empty. He pulled over at the next gas station they came to. A dog was barking, a rusty Coca-Cola sign creaked in the breeze. A thin attendant with bad teeth and a baseball cap limped out toward the pumps. His nose looked like it had been gnawed away by mosquitoes for the last twenty years. He filled up the tank, grinning, and asked Harry if that was who he thought it was in the car. Harry nodded and Duke got out of the car, shook the guy's thin fingers, and watched the happiness spread over his features like dawn over a dilapidated town. Harry said about the car not running so good and the guy peered inside the hood, cigarette ash dropping into the engine as he did so. Duke called himself the world's number one navigator but mechanics was a different matter altogether. The best he could do was stand around and look interested while someone else did the work, watching Harry peer anx-

iously over the guy's shoulder. He tugged a few tubes, wiped some parts, checked the oil and spark plugs, and grunted appreciatively before slamming down the hood and chucking away the cigarette butt.

—Must've just been some bad gas last time you filled up, Duke, he said, wiping his forehead with the back of his hand. Carburetor's fine, oil's fine, don't want nothin doin to it. All she wants is the road.

Harry grinned back at him, relieved and proud as a parent.

Back in the car he honked the horn and Duke waved as they eased back onto the highway.

—Come back anytime, Duke, the guy called after them. Anytime.

He wanted to pull spectac-
ular robberies, driving up to a bank and blasting away,
leaving a couple of innocent bystanders on the floor
and charging out, banknotes surfing to the ground in
the hot gust of exhaust as they roared away. His part-
ners never let him carry a gun; they thought he was
too crazy, and Art, though disappointed, felt a certain
pride that such tough people thought he was so far
gone.

One time he robbed a doctor's place, made off with
some dope and random bottles of pills. With the pills
he thought maybe he and Diane would manage to
clean up. Getting bombed on pills—that was his idea
of cleaning up.

The rooms of the wall retched. One moment he was
weightless as if in space, the next he could feel gravity
reaching up and grabbing his ankle through the boards
and when he hit the floor it felt soft and welcoming
as a pillow. Colors flared and drained. The curtains
were drawn and the lights always on, the bare bulb in
the middle of the room like a white sun that never
moved. Chills like a knife, a viper twitching in his gut.

He looked at Diane and saw just a sack of misery and fluid. Sometimes he'd lash out at her and find all he'd kicked was a vomit-stained cushion. The television always on: sometimes serials, quiz shows, or Western deserts and a sky of high cloud. Other times cars or faces, throbbing, heads in close-up reeling around like a fruit machine: he fiddled with the vertical hold, hoping to see things stabilize but guessing he must have done something wrong because now there was no picture at all, only voices.

Diane whining: Turn it off, Art, turn it off.

By now, though, he was engrossed, staring at the set until something else caught his attention and he stumbled off, foot snagging on the flex of a lamp, and he went over onto the carpet, followed by the small explosion of the lamp going over and smashing. Which meant it was up to Diane to turn the TV off and she fiddled with all the controls, pulling out the aerial finally and turning up the volume so that now there was a constant roar and twitch of molecular sea, a white snow of noise, like some broadcast from another planet. Once she drew the curtain back an inch and in a knife blade of light the colors outside bleached the back of her eyes.

For breakfast they swallowed pills, shaking the bottles when empty, squinting up into them like a telescope pointed at a brown galaxy of light. Also this urge to open and shut things: closets, doors, the fridge, taking the lid off a tub of margarine and then just leaving it.

The toilet was a yellow pond. Sitting on the edge of the bath, he saw his hand snake out and flick the toilet roll so that a pale rope of paper descended to the floor and he kept on doing it, enjoying the sight of the soft tissue piling up on the cold floor. Eventually he got bored doing that and went back to the living room where the floor was a sponge of vomit, blood, and broken glass. Here and there, where flowers should have been, crumpled balls of newspaper slowly breathed and seemed always about to bloom. Sometimes a hot fever in his head and other times his limbs felt so weak that even crossing or uncrossing his legs seemed like a walk over dull hills.

Diane was saying something to him but her words melted into a gray slush of sound. He pictured her lying in a gutter, her body decomposing and a car tire squelching through her like snow. He watched her make her way toward the kitchen, where all the cupboards were flung open as if some gale were passing through the house. Halfway there she sagged over and was caught by the carpet, a triangle of glass protruding from her cheek like a rose thorn and not even noticing the blood that quite suited her anyway.

By now the sofa was where he puked and retched because nothing came up except a slime of bile. His face sticky all the time from something that oozed out of his eyes and nose and felt like a hot snail had crawled across his face. When he woke soft crusts had formed around his eyes, which felt as if they had been shined with a hot rag.

Diane was whining and yelping like a hungry dog and Art realized with a laugh that it *was* the dog—an easy mistake to make given there was no difference between those two bitches anyway. The dog was terrified and Art, back in the storm-tossed kitchen, went through the cupboards, closing and opening everything again. He poured a saucer of milk, knowing this was the right thing to do with cats and hoping it might keep the dog happy too—then spoiling it all by inadvertently standing on the saucer so that there were little pools of milk and an archipelago of blue crockery on the linoleum. He went through the kitchen like someone turning the place over, sweeping through each cupboard with his forearm, sending cans and pots tumbling to the floor and only then looking to see what his search had revealed. He found a can of dog food and then started on the drawers, looking for an opener, holding everything up high above his head and letting knives and forks pour over him like sharp rain clattering to the floor. On his hands and knees he looked through everything, found a can opener and jabbed it into the can's guts, hacking around, ripping his finger on a rough edge and not caring, prizing open the glistening trunk of meat that stuck to the fork, and then just leaving it like that, the dog already chewing.

Back in the main room he fell asleep on the sofa, dreamed of nothing at all, nothing, not even gray or white or any color, nothing at all, with no time or sound but definitely a dream, not like the black weight of sleep. The dream felt like bliss until it became flecked with colors and cold pain and he was awake again, joints like a diver up too fast from twenty fathoms, mouth so dry it felt like there was no liquid in his body anymore, coming around and wondering if that was what it was like to be in a coma. An ache everywhere, as soon as he located it in one place he became aware of a pain more intense somewhere else and so for a while he lay there just tracing the movement of pain around his body, then noticing that he was on the floor, wet with blood, Diane lying unconscious a couple of feet away. His first thought was that he'd killed her and the satisfaction of that was fast superseded by the fear that she really wasn't breathing anymore. Somehow he got up, the blood surging to or from his head, swaying like a tower in the wind, kicked her once and no response, as if he'd just kicked a bag of earth, so again, harder, and this time she twitched and cried quietly.

Then he could take it no more, stormed out of the house, slamming the door behind him but unprepared for how the heat of the outside world poured into him like a succession of punches. At first it was too bright, his eyes bruising in the glare. Then he saw the street and the well-tended squares of lawn, heard the familiar whine of traffic. From then on habit did its work. The next thing he knew he was turning over the engine, hearing the car respond, moving. The mirror he had no use for, all his attention locked on where he was going, what lay ahead. Cars moved past like blurs but at the first intersection there was a jolt and his head slammed into the windshield. The guy in the car in front got out, angry, ready to fight, but when he saw Art, bloodstained, rabid, and smelling of vomit, he paused, unsure of what he might be getting into, and just looked on as this maniac squealed the car around him.

He turned up at the house of some friends, junkies who took one look at him and agreed quickly to give him a hit on credit. Immediately the agony was lost in the elixiric surge of warmth that was almost too strong. He dunked his face in a clear basin of water, borrowed another hit for Diane, and tripped out of the house, repeatedly mumbling his gratitude, making wild promises to pay them back many times over.

By the time he was back on the freeway his veins were lit up by the fast traffic of heroin in his blood, feeling a glow in the pit of his stomach, his vision clearing. He drove cautiously at first but then moved out, passing slower cars until he was burning along, windows down, the hot wind streaming through his hair, his washed face drying quickly, enjoying the spots of water dripping from his nose into his lap, feeling the rush of blue air and moving fast along the freeway, the gray roar of tires, the sun dancing off the white roofs of cars. He jabbed the buttons on the radio, scanning through the stations and stopping suddenly when he came to a jazz station, hearing first of all a trio and then recognizing his own sound as the sax threaded its way forward, slinking and weaving like a red car through light traffic, his foot barely touching the gas pedal, the tone as clear as the long light, sharp as shadows. He turned the radio up until the car was trailing a loud exhaust of sound, reached into the glove compartment and pulled on a pair of dusty shades, enjoying the deepened greenish light that only made the silver rush of the sax seem brighter, more beautiful than before—like a clear hot day, birds moving through a soundless sky. A car winding its way along the twisting coast road, taking the curves slowly, every now and then a brief glimpse of the Pacific until, pulling out of a bend, there is a huge view of the blue ocean stretching away, the bridge like a girdered sunset above it. Waves breaking on rocks and sand. Swooping gulls.

·

High up on one wall the bars of the small window threw zebra stripes of light and shadow across the floor. He paced the cell and glanced at the figure stretched out on the top bunk before slumping down onto the lower bed, the tracks of the shadows falling over him. Head in his hands, elbows on thighs. His left hand reached around his right shoulder, scratching a spot just below the armhole of the sweat-stained singlet before massaging the biceps of each arm with the hand of the other. His legs protruded thin and white from grayish shorts, the unlaced boots on his feet making his legs seem scrawny. All over one wall were pictures torn from *Playboy* of grinning women, pale and naked except for the glisten of lipstick and gold sheets, satin, silk. He stretched out on the bunk, shut his eyes for several minutes, and then climbed off the bed and paced the cell again. Every gesture he made was slow: his movements had shrunk, cramped themselves to the confines of the cell, but they had also expanded to fill the hours that took weeks to pass, the afternoons that felt like months. He glanced at the makeshift calendar taped to one wall as often as a man waiting for a train looks at his watch.

Grasping the bars of the window, he hauled himself up, muscles straining in his arms, a vein swelling in his neck. All he could see was an angle of sky and sun, but pulling himself higher, he could see the refineries and warehouses near the beach. Feet anchored against the wall, trying to ease the weight on his arms, he heaved himself still higher, twisting his head into the angle of wall and ceiling. At least a third of the view was obstructed by the prison wall but, from this difficult perch, he could make out the beach clearly: people lounging in deck chairs, waves slapping in. Scanning further along, he saw an old wharf, a woman, tanned, spreading out a towel and stripping off. She was a long way off but the light was so perfect he could make her out clearly. Slipping out of her blouse and skirt, a red bathing suit underneath. Heat, blue water, spray. She stretched out on the towel. One leg raised, digging into her bag for something—cigarettes, sun lotion . . . He hung for as long as he could and then dropped to the floor, breathing heavily, striped by shadows.

He was walking along the strip of beach he could only glimpse from his cell, the sky bleached by heat. Everyone else was tanned and in shorts, glancing at him as he passed incongruously by in a dark suit, carrying a suitcase and a smaller instrument case. He looked around him all the time, whether through nervousness or fascinated absorption in things was impossible to say. If someone came close he looked to the ground, raising an arm to shade his face from their gaze.

When he came to the wharf he stopped and looked for the woman he saw from the cell. A couple of people were stretched out in the sun but she was not there. Looking around again, he saw her on the beach just beyond the wharf, towel spread out beneath a beach umbrella, talking to a man in his late thirties, maybe slightly older. Wearing a bright short-sleeved shirt that looked like it was bought in France or Europe. Kissed her on the cheek and gathered up his things before walking toward Art, noticing him as he passed by. Art watched his receding figure until, out of the corner of his eye, he caught a glimpse of someone he recognized, padding along the boardwalk in front of a beach café, long legs flapping like a pair of jeans hung out to dry on a windy day. Picking up his cases, Art trotted off behind him, laying a hand heavily on his shoulder.

—Hey, you black motherfucker, where you think you're going? The guy turned around fast, one hand reaching for his back pocket, eyes fierce with anger until he saw Art smiling at him.

—Hey, you white muthafuckah . . .

—How ya doin, Egg?

They shook hands, embraced, pummeling each other on the back, Egg saying:

—I was just gonna carve your face up, man . . . How you doin, Art?

—Good.

—I didn't know you was out.

—Not too many people do. So how you doin?

—Everything cool, man, everything's cool. How was it there after I got out?

—Not the same man.

—Jackie doin OK in there?

—He's making out. He's a tough kid, Egg.

—Yeah. Hey, it's good to see you, Art—thumping him softly on the shoulder.

—You too, man . . . Hey, listen, can I cop from you?

—Man, you don't change. How long you been out? Are we talking days, hours, or what?

—We're talking minutes, man, said Art, smiling; Egg laughed out loud. So can I cop?

—You been out twenty minutes and you already lookin to go straight back, said Egg, shaking his head. Whassamatter with you, man, you like it in stir?

Art smiled again. A game of volleyball had started up near them, surrounding them with the thwack of the ball and shouts. Sand splashing up as the players dived for the ball.

—Why don't you get yourself a different hobby? Volleyball or somethin . . . How much money you got, man? he said at last, tugging at an earlobe with thumb and forefinger.

—Nothing, man. This'll have to be on credit. C'mon, Egg.

—Oh, man, said Egg, shaking his head.

—Get me some works too, can you? said Art, abruptly more serious.

—You tryin to get me busted?

—How soon can you get it?

—Tomorrow afternoon, day after.

—Make it tonight, Egg.

—Man, you do *not* change . . .

—I appreciate it, man.

—Yeah, man.

They shook hands, loosely, already parting as their hands touched.

Picking up his cases again, Art walked back to the woman on the beach. She was lying on her stomach, fidgeting as people do when trying to work in an environment conducive only to idleness. As Art moved closer he made out for the first time details of her appearance: medium-length brown hair, small nose, lips that seemed constantly on the point of smiling. A shadow fell across her page, she glanced over and saw a pair of shoes in the sand, socks, cuffs, a man's besuited knees coming into view as he crouched beside her.

—Hi.

She turned toward him, surprised, irritated, instinctively aware of the inequality of their meeting: she almost naked, he wearing a suit so inappropriate it would have been comic had it not been for the faint air of menace it conveyed.

—Hi, she said quietly, the question "What do you want?" condensed into that one syllable. She looked at him through the hair that had fallen across her eyes leaving strands of shadow on her face, waiting to see what his pitch was going to be. She fingered aside her hair as he stared at the ground, picking up sand and letting it drift through his hands. Watching him, aware already of the tension in him, she remembered reading somewhere that when you are attracted to a man the first things you notice are his fingers. This man's were the exact opposite of elegant: short, broken nails, not even clean. His hair was cropped army-short. Blue-collar looks, handsome but worn out. He looked up, hand shielding his eye from the glare, squinting.

—It's . . . bright, he said at last, clearing his throat, still not looking at her.

She nodded, the expression on her face like someone who has heard a knock at the door, opens it, and finds herself confronted by a complete stranger, someone with no reason to be there.

—That's a pretty towel. Real pretty.

Again she felt an impulse to laugh at the ludicrous-
ness of the comment. Instead, as neutrally as possible,
she said thank you.

—English, huh?

—Yes. That was the way it went: you had to offer
as little as possible in these situations, reduce the conversation to so narrow a base that there was no room
for him to gain any purchase while he tried to build
as much intimacy as possible on the flimsiest of pre-
texts.

—I'm American, he said, not smiling at all.

—How fascinating, she said eventually, glancing
down at her book. As she did so she was aware of him
looking at her body, trying to make it appear that he
was looking out at the breaking surf but all the time
she could feel his eyes drawn back to her, burning on
her like the sun.

—I've seen you before, he said after a while.

—Where?

—Here. You're here most days. Either here or on
the wharf.

—I haven't noticed you.

—No, maybe not.

—She changed position, moved from lying propped
on one elbow to sitting, the leg nearest him drawn up
defensively as a way of putting a barrier between them,
all the time aware that the barrier was her naked leg.

—So, uh, so what you doin here?

—Getting a suntan.

—In California, I mean.

—My husband is teaching a course at the Music
Institute for a year.

Neither of them looking at the other.

—Husband. Man, that's not one of my favorite
words, he said eventually, scraping a trench in the sand
with one finger.

—That the guy who was here just now?

—Yes.

—What's he teach?

—Twentieth-century composition. Modern classical.

—Modern classical, huh?

—Yes.

Was there a wind blowing before? Possibly: a breeze only strong enough to send grains of sand crawling slowly over each other and take a fine spray of mist from the tops of waves. Now there was none, only the stillness of the sky.

—Maybe I could get you a beer? Before he asked he knew she would refuse.

—No, thank you.

—Coffee?

She shook her head, looked again at the Sahara of patterns his finger was forming in the sand.

—Coke?

—No.

—Tea?

—No.

—Tea with milk . . . Lemon tea? . . . Iced tea . . .

—No, really . . .

—How about a milk shake? Strawberry, lemon, banana, vanilla?

—You're very kind but—

—Hey, c'mon, I'm celebrating.

Hesitating, unsure whether to ask or not, surprised to find that she too was tracing patterns in the sand, she paused a moment longer before saying, with exaggerated care:

—What are you celebrating?

—You wanna know?

—No.

—You really wanna know?

—No.

—Well, if you really want to know, I'm celebrating the anniversary of the worst thing that ever happened to me.

She said nothing, made no move. Art gestured at her open-handed, raising his eyebrows, prompting her to ask what it was.

—You want to know what it was?

—No.

—You really wanna know?

—No.

—OK then, I'll tell you since you're so persistent. Five years ago to the day, I'm having dinner with this girl, real nice apartment and everything. Got a plate-glass table, these snazzy wire basket chairs on thin metal legs. Stereo, freezer, everything.

His voice was somewhere between a whine and a drawl, monotonous but impassioned, the voice of someone only interested in what he was saying, a voice you could imagine endlessly justifying his actions, promising and pleading and denying all responsibility for things he had done.

—And she's got these two really cute little chihuahuas and they're scampering around all over the place but real quiet, not barking or anything. Anyway, we dated a few times but this is the first time I've been invited to her apartment. So I take her flowers and chocolate and shit and we're talking and eating, getting on real well and she tells me how she loves her dogs and I kind of ruffle their heads a bit and it gets to the dessert, this fancy ice cream, like about eight flavors rolled together in a ball, and I lean forward, kind of tip forward in my chair with the fancy spindly legs and lean across the see-through table and kiss her just soft on the lips, all cold and sweet from the ice cream. And I say all romantic, "I've been wanting to do that all evening." And she says, "I've been waiting for you to do that all evening." So I'm tipped right forward in the chair and I think what I've got to do is move around to her side of the table, so I lean back in my chair and there's this squishing crunching sound and a yelp and I look down and, man, I've skewered this chihuahua with the metal leg of my chair. The leg has gone right through him like he's some kind of kebab or something you're gonna barbecue but he's not dead, he's just, you know, his eyes are all busting out of his head and his tongue is like wagging . . .

He was smiling and looking at her, watching her laugh.

—So what happened? she asked, coughing through her laughter.

—Well, she's screaming and upset and there's blood all over the floor and we start trying to prize this chihuahua off the chair leg like someone in a Western with an arrow in his chest, you know, trying to pull it out but he's kind of stuck . . .

Ten minutes later she had changed into her blouse and skirt, sitting at a table at the beach café. A waiter brought a tray loaded with bottles, glasses, and cups to her table, the sun glinting off the sharp angles of ice, the thin curves of glass. She paid the waiter, looked briefly at her book, and wondered just what she was getting into. The fact that he had ordered two of everything for himself, two beers, two coffees, two Cokes, and was in the rest room when the waiter brought the drinks—leaving her to pay—was so unsurprising as to seem inevitable. What was surprising was that she was here at all. It was when he made her laugh, that was the turning point. As a child, when she was mad at her brother, yelling at him for some spiteful thing he'd done, he would say to her, "I know you're angry, you're very angry, so whatever you do, don't spoil it by laughing. Don't laugh. Whatever you do, do not laugh." And by that time laughter would be bubbling out of her mouth like soda from a can. It was the same now. Her laughter had got her into this, it was her laughter that betrayed her. Lost in these reflections, she hadn't noticed him returning to the table. He sat down, smiling, poured the beer into a glass, rubbed the bottle over his forehead, took a gulp of beer, and wiped his lips with the back of his hand. She watched him taking another swig—as if nothing outside that glass of beer existed in the world, as if he might actually pass out from the pleasure it gave him. She took a bitter sip of lemon.

—That suntan's really coming along, he said, angling the bottle at her, a fleck of foam on his lips.

—You're very pale.

—Oh yeah, I haven't been in the sun for a while, he said, peeling foil from the top of the bottle.

—How come? She rattled the ice around in her glass, a gesture always designed to make the significant question seem as casual as possible.

—I've been away, out of the country. I've been in, uh, what's that place . . . Denmark? Norway . . . You ever been out there?

—No.

—Aw, you should go, he said, draining the beer, emptying sugar into his coffee, dumping in half the pitcher of cream. There's an awful lot happening up there. The fjords and everything. Cold, though.

She whisked the ice in her drink with the straw, looked up over the sea at a plane skywriting the name of a new restaurant. Looking down again, she saw he had finished the coffee and was now ripping open more packets of sugar, pouring them into his glass of Coke.

—It's a miracle you have any teeth left.

He smiled at her: perfect teeth. Someone had put a record on the jukebox, slow jazz.

—So what were you doing there, in Norway?

—I'm a musician, he said, tracing squiggly patterns in the melted ice and spilled water on the tabletop.

—What kind of music do you play?

—Jazz.

—I thought all jazz musicians were colored.

—Not all.

—But the best ones are, aren't they?

A dagger of anger flashed in his eyes. Always that same claim that he had to pit himself against. If his life had a purpose it was to bury that claim once and for all. Years from now, in New York, he would tell a journalist, without any hint of irony: "In a very short time I'll be like Trane. There was Pres, then Bird, and then Trane. And then there's going to be Pepper. I've felt that way all my life. I've never doubted it." Perhaps that was why, looking straight at her, he felt a strange sense of déjà vu as he said, slowly:

—Nobody plays better than me. Meaning it totally.

—And modest with it. She returned his gaze, a thin smile of lime floated on the surface of her drink. The writing on the sky was fading.

—You like jazz?

—I've never listened to it properly. I heard some Duke Ellington records once and some Charlie Parker . . . Richard—my husband—keeps promising to take me to a concert.

—He's into jazz?

—Not really, she said, laughing through her nose. He says it's undisciplined, too reliant on improvisation.

—And this guy teaches music?

She opened her mouth, there was the sharp intake

of breath that precedes speech, but he went on hurriedly, burying the implied insult:

—You ought to go to one of the clubs. The Hillcrest or one of those joints. You'd like it. Maybe I could take you?

She said nothing.

—Maybe, he said eventually, speaking her lines for her.

—And what instrument do you play?

—Guess.

—Trumpet?

—No.

—Saxophone.

—Yeah, alto.

—And you've made records?

—Not in a while . . . You hear that? he said, gesturing toward the café, the source of the music that breezed around them. That's me playing.

—Really?

—Yeah. She cocked her head to one side, listening.

—Is it really you?

—You don't believe me?

—Is it you?

—Sure. Who else could play the blues like that? he said, laughing.

—I don't know. What is the blues?

—The blues? Man, that's a big question. The blues is a lot of things, a feeling . . .

—What kind of feeling?

—Well, it's . . . Maybe it's a guy alone, locked up some place 'cause he got in some trouble that wasn't his fault. And he's thinking of his girl and how he hasn't heard from her for a long time. And maybe it's visiting day and all the other cats are down there seeing their wives and their girls. And he stays in his cell, thinking about her. Wanting her and knowing he's lost her, hardly able to remember her properly because for a long time all he's seen are the girls pinned on the wall, not like real women at all. Wishing there was somebody waiting for him, thinking how his life is passing by and how he's messed everything up. Wishing he could change everything, knowing he can't . . . That's the blues.

When he had finished speaking she listened even more intently to the music, like someone staring at a photograph of a lover's parent, straining to spot an elusive likeness.

—All that hurt and pain, she said at last. But . . . but . . .

—But what?

—But . . . beautiful. Like kissed tears, she said, smiling at how silly that sounded. Is it really you?

—Can't you tell?

—I don't know you. How can I tell?

—You don't have to know me. You can tell . . . Listen. That's my voice, my hands, my mouth. Everything. It's me.

He took off his jacket. She looked at the barroom tattoos on his arm, looking at him differently now, searching for the source of the music.

As she watched he moved as if to touch her knee but instead of touching her his hand hovered six inches above her skin. Keeping this distance from her, he moved his hand up her leg so that his shadow caressed her thigh.

—You know how long it's been since I was this close to a woman?

She remained completely still, offering nothing, looking beyond him to the beach where two children were trying in vain to launch a kite into the still air. He moved his hand so that its shadow inched up her legs, toward the hem of her skirt, over her stomach. The music faded into nothing and there was only the distant blood-beat of surf.

—You want a woman enough and she wants you, he said.

With each word the shadow moved a fraction of an inch, so slowly as to hardly move at all.

—Sometimes that's true. Not always.

The shadow moved over her breasts, toward her throat.

—It doesn't have to be true always. Just now.

—Sometimes, knowing a man wants you, it makes you despise him. Other times, yes, it makes you want to give yourself to him because you can't bear the thought of all that pain, all that longing. It's too frightening. So his weakness becomes a kind of strength and all your strength becomes weakness. Maybe it will be different one day. Then maybe a woman will see a man somewhere and she'll want him. But now she has to be wanted, she has to know how much he wants her.

His shadow was over the side of her face, he moved his hand closer, touching her hair, pushing it back over one ear.

—And now. You know how much I want you?

He grasped her sunglasses, hooked them off, traced a line down her face and along her lips with the arm of the sunglasses. She squinted in the glare and he put the shades, gently, on the table beside her.

—No.

—What can I do? Can I tell you how you look to me now? Maybe I could tell you about your ankles and your shins, your legs . . . If I was a painter, he said in a poor imitation of an English accent, gesturing extravagantly, I could draw your breasts, your hair. The way the sun catches your throat . . .

—No. She smiled back, relieved that there was still room for laughter.

—Or what I want to do to you. How I want to hold you in my arms and kiss your neck. How I want . . .

She shook her head: —That's not enough.

—But if I could tell you, you'd listen?

—Yes.

—You'd hear how much I want you?

—Yes.

They held each other's gaze until he reached down to the cases on the floor beside him, opened one of them, and quickly assembled the alto, moving his fingers lightly over the keys. Behind him, close to the sea, she saw the children trying again to launch their kite. The first notes he played were so soft they were barely audible over the sound of the surf rolling in behind him. Then his sound lifted clear of the waves like the red kite she saw over his shoulders. He played with his eyes shut and she watched the kite float into the warm sky, twitching in a breeze so slight it seemed insufficient to keep the kite aloft, tugging gently at strings so fine they were invisible. Within minutes the kite hung high overhead, a long tail-streamer flopping lazily after it.

He opened his eyes briefly, saw her held in the trance of the music, and shut his eyes again, playing hard, calling to her through the music, the memory of her face vivid to him . . .

He opened his eyes again, knowing something was still not right in a passage he'd already stumbled over several times before. His hands kept being drawn to a couple of notes which he knew were not right for her—too easy, too obvious. Still, he was getting there, the song was shaping itself around her and soon it would fit her as perfect as her favorite dress. He looked at the photo on the wall, laid his sax on the bunk bed, his head filling up with the carceral clang of metal on metal. He paced the cell again. Looked at the calendar, picked up the horn as if it was the key to the prison, blowing long notes that attempted to fill the cell with the space of the beach and sky, the light and waves sweeping in.

—Hey, why'd you stop, Art? said Egg from the top bunk. That's a nice one . . . Real pretty.

—Yeah, it's gonna be a pretty song.

—What's it about? What's it called?

—I dunno, man. It's about somebody I never even met, it's about what it's gonna be like when I get outta here. How it might be.

—Beautiful, man.

—It's not right yet. It's not her yet.

—Well, she sure sounds hot to me, man. Play another one, Art . . .

—OK, so what you want to hear?

—Anything, man, a ballad, something with a story in it, somethin soft, soft as that beautiful wet pussy I'm gonna get my black hands on the moment I get outta here in exactly two hundred ten and a half days' time.

—Man, the only pussy a black motherfucker like you's gonna get his hands on is one with a tail and claws, a real fucking dog pussy.

—A dog pussy, hah, that's a muthafuckah, man. Maybe you oughta write a song called that, haha. "Dog Pussy Blues." Haha. Hey and I want a percentage for the title on that.

—Man, this shit is wasted on you, Egg . . .

—No, I'm foolin, man, it's beautiful music, beautiful, man. No shit. You know when you're outta here and you play some of those real pretty things and it's on the radio and the guy says that was Art Pepper playing, I don't know, some tune with a chick's name, I'm gonna tell folks: Hey, I was the first muthafuckah to hear that, he wrote it when we were in the joint together.

—Sure, Egg, said Art, smiling and walking over to the small metal table where Egg had left his cigarettes. A deck of cards was next to the smokes. He tapped a cigarette from the pack and cut the deck. Ace of diamonds: a red kite in a window of white sky.

In San Quentin the gray prison fatigues make him feel like an actor performing scenes from the life of Art Pepper. Guards in concrete watchtowers, searchlights, rifles, dogs. The constant possibility of violence. Gray walls, queuing for chow, the sound of a thousand men eating the same food off plastic plates.

Somebody tells him that Cagney is the patron saint of cons. There are times when his sense of filmic self-definition is so strong he imagines he is in Alcatraz. The Rock.

He is lounging in the exercise yard, standing to the side of a small group of black prisoners. The walls throw a frontier of shadow across the yard; it advances imperceptibly across the ground, a slow annexation of the daylight glare.

—That's the thing about prison, a voice says to his right. Even when you're outside you're inside.

He turns to look at the guy who has spoken to him; a black guy he's seen before, a guy people are scared of, whom nobody messes with. Skin soaking up the sunlight, eyes burning in the glare. Art does not quite meet his gaze.

—You're Art Pepper.
—Right.
—The musician.
—Yeah.
—Alto. The great alto player.
—Maybe.

—And junkie.

—That too.

The black guy looks at Art, the face not showing anything, trying to find where the spirit is in him. He looks at the eyes that are already beginning to show the gray flecks of defeat.

—I heard you play a few times.

—In LA?

—Yeah. You played pretty good.

—Thanks.

—For a white man.

He looks closely at Art as he says this but his face gives nothing away, not fear or defiance or pride, not anything. By now his body has become a kind of cell; years of prison have meant that he has evolved a way of always hiding himself so that if he got cut with a knife it wouldn't touch his vital organs. His face is as blank as the prison walls. That expression is the best way of being left alone. In later years his tone will evolve something of this self-protective quality, always enclosed by its own perfection. From now on everything he plays will be touched by the misery of prison and what he learned there.

—You miss playing?

—Yeah.

—How long?

Art shakes his head, almost smiles.

The black guy talks to a thin guy with an Afro and frightened eyes who trots off across the yard. A few minutes later he returns with a dull-looking alto. The first guy takes it and hands it to Art.

—Take us on a trip.

—I haven't touched a horn in a year.

—So now's the time.

—I don't know if I can still play.

—You can play.

The horn is cradled in his arms. He lifts it to a vertical position, feeling the keys rattle against the buttons of his prison tunic. The shadow has crawled to within a couple of feet of him and he steps out of the glare, into the cool. After blowing a few scales he starts to play a simple melody, something he knows well, something he can feel his way by, get used to the mouthpiece, the fingering. Playing slow. A couple of the guys near him click their fingers; he sees a foot moving slightly in the bright yard.

For a couple of minutes he plays nothing but the melody, then begins to move away from it, cautiously at first, careful not to lose himself. He hears someone say his name, is aware that more and more people in the yard are listening, the hubbub of voices subsiding. There is a perfection of space about the way the prisoners are spread out in the yard. Although he is still playing the melody, it is as if it is gradually becoming hemmed in and has less room to move until all it can do is cry out, tearing at itself like someone dashing his head against the walls of a cell.

One of the cons whispers that it is like hearing a man's spirit beaten out of him. Next to him an old Negro shakes his head:

—No, he's gonna break free.

After a flurry of twisted notes it seems there is nowhere for the solo to go. No one moves, the cons stand where they are, surrounding him like a fighter who has been beaten to the canvas, struggling to clear his head. Spitting out slurred notes like broken teeth, preparing to haul himself up the ladder of the referee's count. Listening, the prisoners know that his playing is about something which is not higher but deeper than dignity, self-respect, pride, or love—deeper than the spirit: the simple resilience of the body. Years from now, when his body has become a sustaining reservoir of pain, Art will remember the lesson of this day: if he can stand up he can play, and if he can play he can play beautifully.

For a few moments he falters, oblivious to what he is playing, clutching the eighth and ninth rungs of the count. Then, summoning everything, he searches for the highest note, reaches it—just—and soars clear. At the height of this leap, before gravity reasserts itself, there is a moment of absolute weightlessness—bright, clear, serene—before he is falling again, gliding in a gorgeous arc, subsiding into the deep moan of the blues. And the convicts realize that's what it's been about all along—a dream of falling.

When he finishes he is sweating. He nods his head so slightly it is like a twitch slowed right down. All around him is the silence of the prisoners listening. Not only the prisoners' silence. There is also the gray silence of the guards, watching. A nightstick tapped four-four time into the hard palm of a hand. Toe caps, concrete, the quiet squeal of crushed grit. Soon not even that.

No applause. Every second feels like the moment before the first smack of palm on palm is heard; but instead there is this long note of silence, stretched impossibly like a precipice never quite there. Everyone aware now of the silence in the yard, of the railroad chuff of a piece of machinery in the prison workshop. Aware too that this silence is in appreciation of the music, an act of collective will, that there is always an inescapable dignity about silence; aware of how easily a scream or shout can destroy it. The silence is a visible thing also, captured in time. No one moves because in order for there to be silence in a place like this, time has to stop. Something must happen to break the silence, to release time again. The guards feel the rising tension of moment heaped on moment like a makeshift barricade: to try to pass it may be to incite a riot. So they wait. The silence smolders; the longer it stews, the more violent will be its eventual eruption into noise. From silence to the din of metal, yelling, and flames. The click of a rifle's safety catch would be enough to incite it, serving as it would like the first tentative tick of a clock coming back to life, setting time off. The silence is like a slowly expanding horizon, a view of distance, making the walls of this prison something worthless and petty. Unnoticed and irrelevant, the warden has come out of his office and is standing quietly in shadow.

The prisoners form a map, the contours of their gaze defining the pale figure who is breathing quietly, cradling the rusty alto in his arms, raising a hand to his mouth as he clears his throat.

.

In 1977 he plays his first gig in New York at the Vanguard. He is fifty-two and plays through a swamp of pain that leaves him clutching the horn like a crutch. Visceral stabs of fire, aches that come and go, burying themselves so deep that a numbness is always vaguely there.

Years ago, he used to catch himself thinking about what he was playing, becoming conscious of his own technique, and while this distracted it also reassured because it meant that in between these spasms of self-consciousness he had simply been playing—and he played best when least conscious of what he was doing. At a certain point playing became a wild amnesia of technique. Now, in what he knows are the last years of his life, he is able to achieve an absorption in the music so total he can routinely lose all sense of himself, play beyond and above himself almost automatically. Every note strains toward the consolation of the blues and even simple passages tear at your heart like a great requiem. Aware of this, he feels almost certain of something he has wondered about, suspected, and hoped for a long while—that he didn't squander his talent by getting as fucked up as he did, that as an artist his weakness was essential to him: in his playing it was a source of strength.

·

In June, Laurie arranges an interview with the head psychiatrist of the hospital whose methadone program Art is enrolled in. The history of modern jazz is a history of musicians ending up in rooms like this; the whiteness of the walls and coats like a denial of the dim, nocturnal world of the music. Even while the doctor is talking Art forgets what he is saying. It is like falling asleep for a few seconds every minute or so, or like a few frames being taken out of time. He hasn't been sleeping nights and now it is as if the diurnal rhythm of time has been speeded up so that he alternates between a few minutes of being conscious and thirty seconds of sleep. Flickering. Coke, heroin, methadone, booze—up to a gallon of cheap wine a day, his body finally cracking up under the abuse he'd subjected it to. Illness and surgery have left him mutilated and scarred: his spleen had ruptured and been taken out, then pneumonia, a ventral hernia, something wrong with his liver, his stomach all bruised and bloated out like . . .

—Like what, Mr. Pepper?

—Like, you know, those black bags you put garbage in? Like when one of those gets a split and all the rubbish and shit starts to bulge out through that.

The doctor takes off his glasses, looks at the hair cropped high up on the forehead, the eyes that offer nothing, not even self-pity or pain. Scanning the battered face, the doctor ponders how this is something that happens to all junkies: there comes a point when the face seems suddenly to collapse in on itself, they start looking very old—not just a few years older than they really are but a hundred: in fact they start to look immortal.

Almost reflexively Pepper scans the room for cupboards where there might be pills, bottles of capsules, vials of powder. The doctor is getting nowhere with his questions, which have to get simpler and simpler to elicit any kind of reply; almost anything, it seems, is beyond him or buried so deep there's no getting to it. After forty-five minutes the questions have gotten to be so simple as to barely be questions.

—Mr. Pepper, what month is it?

He thinks about the temperature outside and has a memory that it was warm, mild, blue gauze skies but then is unsure if that is a memory of another memory from a long time ago. He is tempted to take a stab at April but then, even as the word is forming at the back of his mouth, he changes his mind.

—March?

The doctor pauses and then goes on to the next question, interrupted by a cough from Art.

—Did I get that one right? he chuckles. The doctor could easily become irritated by the junkie drawl of this man's voice, as though he can hardly be bothered to form the words to help himself. He wants everything done for him.

—Who is the President of the United States?

There is a long pause, filled by the dust rattle of white blinds as a breeze makes its way through the window.

—That's a tricky one, says Pepper, looking at the desk in case the answer is hidden there, scribbled on the blotting pad or beneath the glass paperweight which throws back a prism-distended reflection of his own face, one eye looming huge. The names of Presidents run through his head, one after another, but so quickly, like a flock of birds, that he is unable to focus on one. He knows the answer vaguely but is unable to be specific. The doctor waits and watches, fascinated by the slow vagaries of this man's thoughts, and then, by some curious empathy, finds his own mind wandering and for a moment he is unsure of the answer to his own question. This man, thinks the doctor when he is once again confident of the President's name, is utterly self-obsessed; it is as if he cannot remember because he cannot bring himself to care about anything outside his own feelings—and so powerful is this self-absorption that the doctor finds himself not repelled by the simple fact of his selfishness—for it is more than that—but, as it were, sucked into the vacuum of this indifference to everything that is not himself.

Colleagues have told him that this man is a great musician, an artist, and the doctor wonders what kind of music—what kind of art—is it that can raise a man as banal as this to the level of greatness? Jazz—for a few moments he lets the word roam around his head and then, coughing into his fist, he fixes his gaze on the man opposite and says:

—Mr. Pepper, I wonder if you could say what jazz means . . . to you, personally, I mean.

—To me?

—Yes.

—I, uh . . . I suppose . . . Bird, Hawk, Train, Pres . . .

He mumbles these nonsense words to himself, like some kind of mantra. The doctor squints at him, unsure if this random combination of nouns is really an attempt to convey information.

—Excuse me?

—Some other cats too, I guess. Hey, I just remembered the President's name, Pres, Lester. Lester Young.

The doctor looks at him fiercely and grunts, convinced now that any further exertions on his part will prove futile: the man exists in a virtual trance of stupidity.

The interview ends with the drawing back of the doctor's chair over soundless linoleum, a shuffling of papers that is as formalized as a boardroom handshake. He explains a few things to the wife who has been sitting quietly, smiling every now and again as if it is the most natural thing in the world that her husband should have no idea what month it is. The patient himself, meanwhile, has resumed his zombie scanning of the room.

The doctor scribbles a few things in his notebook, among them, in handwriting deliberately more knotted than usual, a note reminding himself to track down some of the records this man has apparently made.

—So where exactly we playing, Duke? asked Harry as they waited on lights at the edge of town.

—No idea, Harry. I thought you knew. I just knew the name of the town.

—Aw, Duke . . . I don't believe it. We've done it again.

—Keep driving. Maybe we'll see a poster or run into one of the guys.

They drove on past billboards and tenements, railroad tracks and the dark entrances of thirstless bars. Garage bunting flickered red and white to welcome them. Traffic lights swayed beneath a continent of sky.

It was a run-down town, smelling of dust and sad factories. Most of the signs they came across read "Closed" or "For Rent." After ten minutes of scanning walls for a poster Harry pulled up at a silver-fronted diner and went in to ask. Often in the past when each had mistakenly assumed the other knew the location of the gig, they'd called into places like this to ask if anyone knew where Duke Ellington was playing that night. Usually somebody would know—occasionally someone would recognize him—but often a dinerful of eaters would shake their heads slowly: "Duke who?" It looked like that kind of town, Duke thought to himself as he watched Harry's tall figure disappear into the diner.

While he waited Duke pulled the rearview mirror around to take a look at himself, at the kangaroo pouches under his eyes and the stubble making its daily reappearance around his chin. Thirty minutes from now, an hour at the most, and they'd be in a hotel, time for a few hours' sleep and something to eat, then the show and off again. If he had the chance he'd snatch an hour to try and work on this new piece which he'd been turning over in his mind ever since he'd switched on the radio at dawn. Nothing he wrote ever ended up as it started out but he already had some thoughts about the guys he might base it around—Pres, Monk, maybe Coleman Hawkins or Mingus—and the kind of things he might try and do. Knowing how to begin, who to start with, that was the difficult part. He'd been running through possibilities but no one—not Bird or Pres or Hawk—really gave it the scope he needed. On an impulse he thought he'd do it randomly, turn on the radio and start with whoever was playing at that moment. After all, he'd got the idea from the radio in the first place and if it wasn't somebody he liked he could ignore it and try again, keep turning on the radio until the right person turned up. It was a crazy idea but what the hell, he'd try it anyway. Wondering who it would be, he flipped the switch and immediately recognized the opening bars of "Caravan"; he glanced at the mirror and saw the answer, smiling and tired, staring him in the face. A moment later he saw Harry, also smiling, emerging from the diner and heading to the car.

—Wrong town completely, Duke . . .

AFTERWORD:

TRADITION,

INFLUENCE, AND

INNOVATION

In his book *Real Presences*, George Steiner asks us to "imagine a society in which all talk about the arts, music and literature is prohibited."[1] In such a society there would be no more essays on whether Hamlet was mad or only pretending to be, no reviews of the latest exhibitions or novels, no profiles of writers or artists. There would be no secondary, or parasitic, discussion—let alone tertiary: commentary on commentary. We would have, instead, a "republic for writers and readers" with no cushion of professional opinion-makers to come between creators and audience. While the Sunday papers presently serve as a substitute for the experiencing of the actual exhibition or book, in Steiner's imagined republic the review pages would be turned into listings: catalogues and guides to what is about to open, be published, or be released.

What would this republic be like? Would the arts suffer from the obliteration of this ozone of comment?

[1] George Steiner, *Real Presences* (Chicago: University of Chicago Press, 1989), p. 4.

Certainly not, says Steiner, for each performance of a Mahler symphony (to stick for a moment to his own preferred terrain) is also a critique of that symphony. Unlike the reviewer, however, the performer "invests his own being in the process of interpretation."[2] Such interpretation is automatically *responsible* because the performer is answerable to the work in a way that even the most scrupulous reviewer is not.

Although, most obviously, it is not only the case for drama and music; all art is also criticism. This is most clearly so when a writer or composer quotes or reworks material from another writer or composer. All literature, music, and art *"embody an expository reflection on, a value judgment of, the inheritance and context to which they pertain"* (my italics).[3] In other words it is not only in their letters, essays, or conversation that writers like Henry James reveal themselves also to be the best critics; rather, *The Portrait of a Lady* is itself, among other things, a commentary on and a critique of *Middlemarch*. "The best readings of art are art."[4]

No sooner has Steiner summoned this imaginary republic into existence than he sighs, "The fantasy I have sketched is only that."[5] Well, it's not. It is a real place and for much of the century it has provided a global home for millions of people. It is a republic with a simple name: jazz.

•

Jazz, as everyone knows, grew out of the blues. From the beginning it developed through the shared participation of a community of audiences and performers.

[2] Ibid., p. 8.
[3] Ibid., p. 11.
[4] Ibid., p. 17.
[5] Ibid., p. 21.

Those like Charlie Parker who went to hear Lester Young and Coleman Hawkins in Kansas City in the 1930s got a chance to blow with them at after-hours jam sessions later the next morning. Miles Davis and Max Roach served their apprenticeship first by listening to and then by sitting in with Parker at Minton's and the Fifty-second Street clubs, learning as they went along. In their turn John Coltrane, Herbie Hancock, Jackie McLean, and dozens of others who went on to school many of the leading players of the 1970s and 1980s learned their trade, as McLean put it, "in the university of Miles Davis."[6]

Because jazz has continued evolving in this way, it has remained uniquely in touch with the animating force of its origins. From time to time in his solos a saxophonist may quote from other musicians, but every time he picks up his horn he cannot avoid commenting, automatically and implicitly, even if only through his own inadequacy, on the tradition that has laid this music at his feet. At its worst this involves simple repetition (those interminable Coltrane imitations); sometimes it involves exploring possibilities that were previously only touched upon. At its best it expands the possibilities of the form.

The focus of these endeavors is frequently one of a number of tunes which have served jazz, throughout its history, as springboards for improvisation. Often these tunes have inauspicious origins as light pop songs. Alternatively, original compositions become standards (in what other medium would a classic be a standard? Imagine Tolstoy published as a Penguin Standard). Thelonious Monk's "Round Midnight" has probably been played by every jazz musician on earth;

[6] Quoted by A. B. Spellman, *Four Lives in the Bebop Business* (New York: Limelight, 1985), p. 209.

each subsequent version tests it, finds out if there is still anything that can be done with it. Successive versions add up to what Steiner calls a "syllabus of enacted criticism."[7] No other art form more ravenously investigates T. S. Eliot's famous distinction between that which is dead and that which is already living.[8]

Ideally, a new version of an old song is virtually a recomposition and this labile relation between composition and improvisation is one of the sources of jazz's ability to constantly replenish itself. Writing on the "Appassionata" piano sonata op. 57, Theodor Adorno notes that "it makes sense to think that what occurred to Beethoven first was not the main theme as it appears in the exposition but that all-important variant of it in the coda, and that he, as it were, retrospectively derived the primary theme from its variation."[9] Something very similar happens frequently in jazz: in the course of a solo a musician touches momentarily and almost accidentally on a phrase which may become the basis for a new tune which will also be improvised on—and these solos may in turn yield another phrase to be developed into a composition. Duke Ellington's musicians frequently grumbled that some lick they'd played in a solo had been noted by Duke and built into a tune published under his name—though they were quick to concede that only someone with Duke's genius could have grasped the potential of that phrase and made as much out of it as he did.

Since he is the most fertile source, we can begin with

    [7] Steiner, *Real Presences*, p. 20.

    [8] T. S. Eliot, "Tradition and the Individual Talent," *Selected Prose* (New York: Harcourt, Brace, 1975), p. 44.

    [9] Theodor Adorno, *Aesthetic Theory* (London: Routledge & Kegan Paul, 1984), p. 249.

Ellington in a more explicit illustration of the way in which the music offers the best commentary on itself. Ellington wrote "Take the Coltrane" for the great tenor player; Charles Mingus' "Open Letter to Duke" is a musical essay on Ellington; it has since been followed by the Art Ensemble of Chicago's "Charlie M." In years to come this chain will almost certainly be lengthened by a homage to Art Ensemble saxophonist "Joseph J" or an "Open Letter to Roscoe" (Mitchell).

This kind of party game could be continued indefinitely, taking various names as our starting point. Thelonious Monk or Louis Armstrong are especially fruitful places to begin but there are literally hundreds of musicians who have had one or two songs written for them. If we drew lines between all available songs in a kind of flow diagram of homages and tributes the paper would soon become impenetrably black, the meaning of the diagram obscured by the quantity of information it would have to convey.

A less explicit strand in the ongoing process of enacted criticism is at work in the evolution of jazz musicians' individual styles. To have a sound and style that are unmistakably your own is a prerequisite of greatness in jazz. Here, as is often the case in jazz, an apparent paradox is at work: to sound like themselves musicians begin by trying to sound like someone else. Looking back to his early years, Dizzy Gillespie said: "Each musician is based on someone who went before, and eventually you get enough of your own things in your playing, and you get a style of your own."[10] Miles Davis in turn tried to sound like Dizzy, and countless trumpeters after him—Wynton Marsalis

[10] Quoted in Ira Gitler, *Swing to Bop: An Oral History of the Transition in Jazz in the 1940s* (New York: Oxford University Press, 1985), p. 56.

most recently—have tried to sound like Miles. Often musicians arrive at their own sound by default. Dizzy again: "All I ever did was try to play like [Roy Eldridge], but I never quite made it. I'd get all messed up 'cause I couldn't get it. So I tried something else. That has developed into what became known as bop."[11] Miles's lonely, chillingly beautiful sound came about as a result of his inability to sustain the high-register leaps that were Dizzy's trademark.

There are two apparently contradictory ways in which the antecedent's voice makes itself heard. Some musical personalities are so strong, so closely associated with a certain sound that they colonize a whole area of expression, and others can encroach on it only at the price of surrendering their individuality. The personality of one musician can so pervade a certain style that it only seems possible to imitate that style, never to adequately absorb or transcend it. It is now almost impossible for a trumpeter to play a ballad with a Harmon mute and not sound as if he is imitating Miles Davis.

Alternatively, there are rare instances of musicians assimilating their predominant influences to such an extent that they seem at times, as Harold Bloom has said of some poets, to "achieve a style that captures and oddly retains priority over their precursors, so that the tyranny of time almost is overturned, and one can believe for startled moments, that they are being *imitated by their ancestors*" (italics in original).[12] Lester Young frequently sounds as if he is indebted to those like Stan Getz who in fact owe their sound entirely to

[11] Quoted in Nat Shapiro and Nat Hentoff, *Hear Me Talkin' to Ya* (New York: Dover Press, 1955), p. 347.

[12] Harold Bloom, *The Anxiety of Influence* (New York: Oxford University Press, 1973), p. 141.

him. At times early Keith Jarrett makes us wonder if Bill Evans does not sound too much like Jarrett.[13]

By the nature of its style of performance jazz affords more opportunities for exactly this kind of comparison than any other art form. The distinction between a group performance and a jam session has always been hazy (a band for a studio date is often flung together at the last moment and even "named" groups are temporary shifting units, rarely demanding the exclusive commitment of any members), and in the course of a year many different musicians will play together in many different formats: duets, trios, quartets, big bands. At its worst this involves a touring star player teaming up with a new pickup rhythm section in each town he plays; alternatively a bassist gets a steady flow of work because he can be depended on to provide solid if uninspired support with minimum rehearsal time. The great advantage of this flexible style of employment, though, is that the individual voices of jazz are heard together in an almost infinite number of permutations, each giving rise to a new collective sound. What would Gerry Mulligan and Monk sound like together? Or Coltrane and Monk? Duke Ellington and Coleman Hawkins? Johnny Dyani and Don Cherry? Don Cherry and John Coltrane? Art Pepper with Miles Davis' rhythm section? Sonny Rollins with Coltrane's? You have only to listen to the records to find out.[14] Every different combination gives a sharper

[13] Cf. Bloom on Wallace Stevens and John Ashbery, ibid., p. 142.

[14] The number of encounters between diverse musicians is great but, of course, there are many musical meetings one wishes had taken place but which didn't: Pharoah Sanders with Johnny Dyani, Dyani and Jarrett, Art Pepper and Jarrett . . . However, the output of musicians like these is so extensively documented that it is not difficult to imagine what such encounters *might* have sounded like. A task for future technology?

sense of the particular qualities of each musician (especially on a record like "Tenor Madness" when Coltrane and Rollins, aged thirty and twenty-seven, respectively, sound almost identical—but how revealing that "almost" proves to be).

When the combinations involve not contemporaries but musicians of different eras playing with each other the results are perhaps even more fascinating. Ellington and Coltrane; Ellington with Mingus and Roach; Milt Hinton and Branford Marsalis. Also documented on record are many encounters where master and pupil—father and son in the case of Von and Chico Freeman—come together again on equal terms: Coleman Hawkins and Sonny Rollins, Ben Webster and Hawkins, Dizzy and Miles.

One of the standard procedures of literary criticism is to juxtapose texts by different authors in order to bring out the particular qualities and relative merits of each. In jazz the constant network of cross-performances means that that task is implicit and inherent in the accumulating catalogue of the music. The performance of a given player simultaneously answers certain questions (about musicians he is playing with or who have come before, about his relation to the developing tradition) and raises other questions (about what he himself is doing, about his own worth, about the form he's working in); the musicians he works with and who come after him provide provisional answers but these answers are also questions—about the worth of *these* musicians, *their* relation to tradition. In an elaborate critical kind of circular breathing, the form is always simultaneously explaining and questioning itself.

With the music itself performing so many of the tasks normally left to commentators, it is not surprising that the contribution of critics to jazz has been relatively insignificant. Of course there are jazz critics and jazz journals. Historically, however, writing on jazz has been of such a low standard, has failed so signally to convey any sense of the animating dynamics of the music as to be irrelevant except—and this is just as Steiner would have it—insofar as it conveys facts: who played with whom, when a given album was recorded, etc. To strip the Western literary or art-historical tradition of criticism would be to decimate our cultural capital (no Berger on Picasso, no Benjamin on Baudelaire). All that has ever been written about jazz, on the other hand, with the exception of musicians' memoirs and the odd jazz-inspired novel (Michael Ondaatje's *Coming Through Slaughter* is a masterpiece), could be lost without doing any but the most superficial damage to the heritage of the music.[15]

2

Despite all that has been said above, jazz is anything but a hermetic form. What makes it a vital art form is its astonishing ability to absorb the history of which it is a part. If no other evidence survived, some computer of the future could probably reconstruct the whole his-

[15] There may be little first-rate writing on jazz but few art forms have been better served by photographers. Indeed, pictures of jazz musicians are virtually the only photographic evidence we have of people engaged in the actual creation of art. This is not to say that actors, singers, or classical musicians are not artists but, however innovative or original, their work is essentially interpretive. Of course there are photographs of composers at their pianos, artists at their easels, writers at their desks, but these are almost always posed—desk, easel, or piano serving as a prop rather than a tool. A photograph of a jazz musician in full flight can bring us as close to the act—or vicarious essence—of artistic creation as a photograph of an athlete can to the act—or vicarious essence—of running.

tory of black America from the jazz catalogue. I am not even thinking of explicit works like Ellington's *Black, Brown and Beige*, conceived as a tone-parallel to the history of African-Americans; Archie Shepp's "Attica Blues" or "Malcolm, Malcolm, Semper Malcolm"; Mingus' "Prayer for Passive Resistance"; or Max Roach's *Freedom Now Suite*. I intend something more general, along the lines suggested by Adorno's observation that "it is not for nothing that the newly soulful tone of the violin counts among the great innovations of the age of Descartes."[16] Elaborating on Adorno, Fredric Jameson comments that "throughout its long ascendancy, indeed, the violin preserves this close identification with the emergence of individual subjectivity."[17] Adorno was referring to the period from the seventeenth century onward but his words are equally applicable to the trumpet's identification with the emergence of black American consciousness in the twentieth century, from Louis Armstrong through to Miles Davis. From the 1940s onward that identification has been rivaled and complemented by the saxophone. According to Ornette Coleman, "the best statements Negroes have made, of what their soul is, have been on tenor saxophone."[18]

Although Coleman is here distinguishing primarily between the tenor and alto saxophones his claim also holds true for a larger distinction between the tenor and other means of expression: literature, painting. This is important, for hand in hand with jazz's capacity to absorb its surrounding history goes its capacity to raise to the level of genius those who would otherwise

[16] Quoted by Fredric Jameson, *Marxism and Form* (Princeton: Princeton University Press, 1971), p. 14.

[17] Ibid., p. 14.

[18] Quoted in Spellman, *Four Lives in the Bebop Business*, p. 102.

have lacked a medium to express themselves. Jazz, as Eric Hobsbawm observes, "has been able to draw upon a wider reservoir of potential artists than any other art in our century."[19] Ellington was a talented painter but many of the other giants of jazz were dependent, in their work, on exactly those qualities and idiosyncrasies which would have hampered their progress in other arts. All the traits that made Mingus' music the wild unpredictable thing it was made the writing in his autobiography, *Beneath the Underdog*, sloppy, foolish. He had nothing of the clerk in him and all writers need something of the pettiness of the clerk, the diligence of the proofreader. "Louis Armstrong without his trumpet is a rather limited man," notes Hobsbawm. "With it he speaks with the precision and compassion of the recording angel."[20] In what other art form could a man like Art Pepper have achieved the beauty he did?

The mention of Pepper is apposite since it reminds us that although primarily, jazz is not exclusively a medium of expression for black experience (as the title of Ellington's *Black, Brown and Beige* indicates, the history of black Americans is inextricably tangled up with that of white America; the Black Nationalist movement was a negative proof of that). The white bandleader Stan Kenton extended the terms of debate still further, hearing in jazz the potential for expressing the anguished spirit of the age: "I think the human race today may be going through things it never experienced before, types of nervous frustration and thwarted emotional development which traditional

[19] Eric Hobsbawm, *The Jazz Scene* (New York: Pantheon, 1993), p. 219 (originally published under the pseudonym Francis Newton in 1959).

[20] Ibid., p. 219.

music is entirely incapable of not only satisfying but expressing. That's why I believe jazz is the new music that came along just in time."[21]

If there is something a little self-serving about Kenton's words—a tacit advertisement for his own music—we can turn instead to a figure of considerable authority who had no vested interest in music. In 1964 Dr. Martin Luther King, Jr., gave the opening address to the Berlin Jazz Festival, his presence there serving as a reminder of how the black people's struggle for civil rights was paralleled by jazz musicians' struggle to have their art recognized as such. In his speech King noted the role played by music in articulating the suffering, hopes, and joys of the black experience long before the task was undertaken by writers and poets. Not only was jazz central to the lived experience of Negroes, he went on, but "in the particular struggle of the Negro in America there is something akin to the universal struggle of modern man."

This is a vital connection; once it has been made jazz becomes a medium representative not only of a people but, implicitly, of a century, a medium that expresses not simply the condition of the black American but a condition of history.

3

"In the middle of a long or at the end of a short life . . ."
JOSEPH BRODSKY

King's remark also nudges us toward an understanding of why a sense of danger—of risk—surrounds the history of jazz.

Anyone who becomes interested in jazz is struck very

---

[21] Quoted in Shapiro and Hentoff, *Hear Me Talkin' to Ya*, p. 385.

early on by the high casualty rate of its practitioners. Even someone not especially interested will probably have heard of Chet Baker, who has become the archetype of the doomed jazz musician, the collapse of his once handsome face serving as a convenient expression of the symbiotic relation of jazz and drug addiction. Of course countless black—and a few white—jazz musicians more abundantly gifted than Chet had lives that were infinitely more tragic (Chet after all was able to live on in the wake of his legend).[22]

Virtually all black musicians were subject to racial discrimination and abuse (Art Blakey, Miles Davis, and Bud Powell were all badly beaten by police). While the likes of Coleman Hawkins and Lester Young who dominated jazz in the 1930s ended up as alcoholics, the generation of musicians who forged the bebop revolution in the 1940s and consolidated its development in the 1950s fell victim to a virtual epidemic of heroin addiction. Many cleaned up eventually—Rollins, Miles, Jackie McLean, Coltrane, Art Blakey—but the list of those who were never addicted would make up a far less impressive roster of talent than those who were. Drug addiction led directly (in the cases of Art Pepper, Jackie McLean, Elvin Jones, Frank Morgan, Rollins, Hampton Hawes, Chet Baker, Red Rodney, Gerry Mulligan, and others) and indirectly (in the cases of Stan Getz, who was caught holding up a store, and Thelonious Monk, who was not using heroin himself) to jail. The route to the psychiatric wards of hospitals, while a good deal more tortuous, was just as well trodden. Monk, Mingus, Young, Parker, Powell,

---

[22] See, for example, Spellman's account of Herbie Nichols, in *Four Lives in the Bebop Business*, pp. 153–77; or Joe "King" Oliver's letters to his sister in Shapiro and Hentoff, *Hear Me Talkin' to Ya*, pp. 186–87.

Roach—so many of the leading figures of the 1940s and 1950s suffered some kind of breakdown that it is only a slight exaggeration of perspective to say that Bellevue has an almost equal claim to Birdland as being the home of modern jazz.

Students of literature routinely see the early deaths of Shelley and Keats, aged thirty and twenty-six respectively, as fulfilling the doomed caveat of the Romantic agony. In Schubert as well we see the essential type of the Romantic talent, consuming itself even as it flourishes. In all three the suggestion is that premature death is a condition of creativity. They sensed that time was running out and their talent had to blossom in a few short years rather than mature steadily over three decades.

For jazz musicians of the bebop era making it into middle age begins to seem like a dream of longevity. John Coltrane died at forty, Charlie Parker at thirty-four; toward the end of their lives both said that musically they did not know where to go next. Many others have died either at the height of their powers or before the full potential of their talent had been realized. Lee Morgan died when he was thirty-three (shot while performing at a club), Sonny Criss killed himself when he was thirty-nine, Oscar Pettiford died when he was thirty-seven, Eric Dolphy when he was thirty-six, Fats Navarro when he was twenty-six, Booker Little and Jimmy Blanton when they were twenty-three.

In a few cases their talent was so prodigious that at the time of their deaths some musicians had already produced an important body of work—but even this consolidated achievement painfully emphasizes how much might have been accomplished in the years to come. Clifford Brown had already established himself as one of the great trumpeters of all time when he was killed in a car crash aged twenty-five (along with pianist Richie Powell, Bud's brother); when you consider that if Miles Davis had died at a similar age there would be nothing beyond *The Birth of the Cool*, some sense of the scale of the loss appears.

Given the lifestyle—drink, drugs, discrimination, grueling travel, exhausting hours—a life expectancy slightly less than that of someone engaged in a more sedate walk of life is to be expected. But still the damage wrought on jazz musicians is such that you wonder if there is not something else, something in the form itself which exacts a terrible toll from those who create it. That the Abstract Expressionists' work somehow impelled them toward self-obliteration—Rothko slashing his wrists over the canvas; Pollock drunk-driving into a tree—is an art-historical commonplace. In the literature of the same period the idea that some inexorable logic in the poetry of Sylvia Plath drove her to suicide, that Robert Lowell's and John Berryman's madness constituted—to borrow the title of Jeremy Reed's study of the phenomenon—"the price of poetry," is just as persuasively familiar. Whatever we make of such ideas, Abstract Expressionism and "confessional" poetry are just interludes in the larger time scale of modern painting and poetry. What then of jazz, which, from the moment of its inception, has apparently wreaked havoc on those who play it? Universally regarded as the first jazz man, Buddy Bolden went mad during a parade and spent the last twenty-four years of his life in a mental asylum. "Bolden went crazy," said Jelly Roll Morton, "because he really blew his brains out through the trumpet."[23]

If at first it seems melodramatic to suggest that there is something inherently dangerous in the form, a little

---

[23] Quoted by Alan Lomax, *Mr. Jelly Roll* (Berkeley: University of California Press, 1950), p. 60.

consideration is likely to leave us wondering how it could be otherwise. Dizzy Gillespie's remark—there's only one way this music is going and that's forward—could have been made at any time this century, but from the 1940s onward jazz advanced with the power and ferocity of a fire sweeping through a forest. How could an art form have developed so rapidly and at such a pitch of excitement without exacting a huge human toll? If jazz has a vital connection with "the universal struggle of modern man" how could the men who create it not bear the scars of that struggle?

·

One of the reasons jazz has evolved so fast is that musicians have been obliged, if for no other reason than to earn decent money, to play night after night, two or three shows a night, six or seven nights a week. Not just to play but to improvise, to invent as they play. This has some apparently contradictory results. Rilke waited ten years for the gale of inspiration that led him to begin the *Duino Elegies* to sweep through him again and enable him to complete them. For jazz musicians there is no question of waiting for inspiration to strike. Inspired or not, they have to get on with the job of making music. Paradoxically, then, the commitment to nightly improvisation, on record dates and in clubs, leads weary musicians to play safe, to rely on tried and tested formulas.[24] Yet the demands of constant improvisation mean that jazz musicians are in a state of constant creative alert, of habitual readiness to invent. On a given night the playing of any member of a quartet can be sufficiently energetic to lift the performances

[24] Cf. Ted Gioia, *The Imperfect Art* (New York: Oxford University Press, 1988), p. 128.

of the rest of the group until a reciprocal shiver passes through audience and performers alike: suddenly the music is *happening*. The working conditions of jazz musicians, moreover, have meant that a vast amount of material has been available for recording (each year dozens of previously unheard performances by the likes of Coltrane and Mingus find their way onto disk). Much of this material sounds fairly ordinary after a couple of listenings—but even while thinking this you are struck also by how high the standard of the average is. Or rather, for the corollary of that observation is the crucial one, you are struck by how high the standards generated by this music are, how quickly you become indifferent to anything that is not touched by greatness. The feeling jazz creates when it is really happening is so subtly but unmistakably different from when the band is just swinging along that large parts of the jazz catalogue (and many live performances) pall by comparison. This knowledge—this feeling—confronts jazz musicians with a steep and daunting slope, especially when so much of what constitutes greatness in jazz lies beyond the range of technique; especially when, as all musicians have agreed, you have to put everything of yourself into your playing, when the music is dependent on your experience, on what you have to offer as a man. "Music is your own experience, your thoughts, your wisdom," said Charlie Parker. "If you don't live it, it won't come out of your horn."[25] Many musicians of the bebop era—Red Rodney is the best example—turned to heroin because they hoped it would put them in touch with whatever it was that longtime addict Charlie Parker drew on for his seemingly endless capacity for musical invention. It is sim-

[25] Quoted in Shapiro and Hentoff, *Hear Me Talkin' to Ya*, p. 405.

ilar to the situation that now prevails in athletics, where competitors take performance-enhancing drugs because the standards of their event seem to exceed that which is attainable without chemical assistance.

By the 1950s young players found that many of Parker's innovations were within their grasp. So abundant was the expressive potential unleashed by Parker that to become fluent in the idiom he had forged was enough to establish a player's reputation. Such a situation is common to all the arts: in painting the potential of Cubism was sufficient to raise the quality of many painters' work to a level above that which they would have been capable of attaining had they been responsible for finding a style through their own efforts. Moreover, the players who rose to prominence initially were those like Johnny Griffin who displayed the peculiarities of bebop—speed in Griffin's case—more markedly than those who strayed from its path.[26]

Toward the end of the 1950s, however, bebop's capacity for nurturing its young came to an end as jazz once again entered a period of rapid transition. Prior to this, as Ted Gioia points out, players were satisfied with making a contribution to the music, finding their own sound on their instrument. By 1960 musicians began to talk as though they were responsible to the music as a whole—not only to its past, to the tradition, but to its future.[27] Tomorrow became the Question, what mattered was the Shape of Jazz to Come. The 1960s saw the stakes raised again as two currents became apparent. Musicians began to see themselves as pushing back the frontiers of the music in an attempt to make it ever more expressive. "I have lived more

---

[26] Cf. Adorno on Pissarro in the era of Impressionism, in *Aesthetic Theory*, p. 36.
[27] Cf. Gioia, *The Imperfect Art*, p. 72.

than I can express in bebop terms,"[28] said Albert Ayler, whose music broke the back of the jazz tradition. Where they were actually trying to take the music may not have been very clear—for the other tendency in the 1960s was for musicians to let themselves be swept on by the accumulated energy of the increasingly spontaneous production of music.

The new music—as it became known—seemed all the times to be moving toward a scream, as if it had internalized the danger that had once been attendant on the production of jazz. As the civil rights movement gave way to Black Power and America's ghettos erupted in riots, so all the energy, violence, and hope of the historical moment seemed to find their way into the music. Simultaneously the music became less a test of musicianship or, as in bebop, of experience and more a test of the soul, of the saxophone's ability to tear out the spirit within. Commenting on the new addition to his band, Pharoah Sanders, Coltrane emphasized not his playing but his "huge spiritual reservoir. He's always trying to reach out to truth. He's trying to allow his spiritual self to be his guide."[29]

4

That Coltrane's name should come up at this point is not surprising. All of the currents mentioned above can be *heard* converging in him. The sense of danger which is inherent and inevitable in the wildfire evolution of jazz becomes audible in Coltrane. From the

[28] Quoted in "The Truth Is Marching In: An Interview with Albert and Don Ayler" by Nat Hentoff, *Down Beat* (November 17, 1966), p. 40.

[29] Quoted by Nat Hentoff in the sleeve notes to John Coltrane's *Live at the Village Vanguard Again!* (Impulse).

early 1960s until his death in 1967 Coltrane sounds as if he is both urging his music forward and being lashed on by it. He was a consummate bebop player who was constantly straining to break free of the confines of existing forms. In the five years it was together the classic quartet of Coltrane, Elvin Jones, Jimmy Garrison, and McCoy Tyner—the greatest creative relationship between four men there has ever been— hauled jazz to a pitch of expressivity that has rarely been exceeded by any other art form. It is Coltrane who takes the lead, but he is utterly dependent on the rhythm section, who not only follow him through his labyrinthine improvisations with split-second responsiveness but force him on to greater exertions. An extreme exploration of the potential of the form seems barely adequate to contain the force and intensity of the spirit of the man in whom the music has its origin. In their last recordings we hear the quartet aching on the frontier of the possible, a highly evolved musical form being taken to its limit (Coltrane, as we shall see, did not stop there).

A key album in Coltrane's musical ascent of the spirit, *A Love Supreme*, closes with a long dream of immanence, a search for an ending that leaves the tenor drifting like smoke over the rhythm section. *First Meditations (for Quartet)*, an album recorded six months later in May 1965, *begins* with that desire to end: there is nowhere for the quartet to go but still they are forcing their way forward. The whole of one side is a painful valediction, the four members of the quartet saying farewell: to each other, to cohesion, to the idea of the quartet as a form capable of containing Coltrane's relentless spirit.

That there is a terrible beauty in the performances of *First Meditations (for Quartet)* and the similar *Sun Ship* (August 1965) is obvious on a first listening. I did not realize how terrible until I heard Pharoah Sanders playing "Living Space" (originally recorded by Coltrane in February 1966) in a duet with pianist William Henderson. Although not quite as raw, Pharoah's sound has all the intensity and passion of Coltrane's but it is serene in a way that Coltrane never is in his last years. I wondered why (criticism, after all, is really only an attempt to articulate your emotions), and soon realized that the reason had to do with Elvin Jones. As it evolved, so the quartet sound came to be dominated increasingly by what were essentially battles between Coltrane and Jones, whose drums are like a wave that never quite breaks, that never stops breaking. As early as 1961, at the close of "Spiritual," the soprano seems about to be drowned by the weight of drums but then emerges again, floating clear of the tidal wave of percussion crashing over it. By the time of *Sun Ship*, especially on "Dearly Beloved" and "Attaining," Jones is murderous: it seems impossible that the saxophone can survive the pounding of the drums. Coltrane is on the cross, Jones is hammering in the nails. Prayer turns to scream. If Jones sounds as though he wants to destroy him, then Coltrane certainly wanted—needed—him to try. Indeed, Coltrane wanted Jones to go even further, and for a while he pitted himself against two drummers: Jones and Rashied Ali, who was ostensibly an even wilder player. Coltrane's last recordings were duets with Ali, but his relationship to Coltrane does not have the same sense of relentless compulsion as Jones's.

At various times Coltrane had used musicians like Eric Dolphy to supplement the core sound of the quartet. From 1965 onward he continually added extra musicians, swamping the quartet and arriving at an almost impenetrable density of sound, rejecting the quartet version of *First Meditations* in favor of a more extreme one featuring Pharoah Sanders and Rashied Ali. Uncertain of what their own contribution could be in such a format, Tyner left in December 1965, Elvin Jones three months later. "At times I couldn't hear what I was doing—matter of fact I couldn't hear what anybody was doing!" said Jones. "All I could hear was a lot of noise. I didn't have any feeling for the music, and when I don't have any feelings, I don't like to play."[30]

In much of Coltrane's last phase (the core group consisting of Garrison, Ali, Sanders, and Alice Coltrane on piano) there is little beauty but much that is terrible. It is music that is both conceived and best listened to in extremis. While Coltrane's concerns were becoming ever more religious, his music for the most part presents a violent landscape filled with chaos and shrieks. It is as if he was attempting to absorb all the violence of his times into his music in order to leave the world more peaceful. Only occasionally, as in the haunting "Peace on Earth," does he finally seem able to partake of the repose he hoped to create.

5

As free jazz disintegrated into what seemed more and more like noise and less and less like music, so the audience for it diminished and increasing numbers of musicians turned to jazz-rock. After what many regard as the dark age of 1970s fusion, the 1980s saw a revival of interest as bop-derived jazz reasserted its hold on a new generation of listeners and performers. Jazz will never be music for a mass audience and its practitioners' lives are still financially precarious, but the danger

[30] Quoted by Val Wilmer in *As Serious as Your Life* (New York: Serpent's Tail, 1992), p. 42.

which was attendant on the creation of bebop and which was internalized in the new music of the 1960s is no longer there. Since that urgent sense of risk was inherent to the feeling of jazz, does this mean that the music has also lost some of its animating force? What is the situation of jazz today?

Compared with the other musics available jazz today is too sophisticated to articulate the lived experience of the ghetto; hip-hop does that better. While it used to be jazz that best expressed the syncopated rhythm of New York, now the city moves to the beat of house. While beats, hipsters, and Mailer's white Negroes were drawn instinctively to jazz as music of rebellion, jazz is increasingly something people arrive at after becoming bored with the banality of pop music. Certainly for the new wave of black British musicians jazz has the status of what Roland Kirk used to call black classical music.

The circumstances in which jazz is performed have also changed. While a few clubs—in New York the Village Vanguard is the best example, the Knitting Factory a more recent one—are devoted entirely to the music, shunning expensive trappings and leaving it to audience and performers to generate atmosphere, the lavishly upholstered supper club has increasingly become the norm. Sometimes a "quiet" policy means that the musicians do not have to compete with too much dinner-table chat to make themselves heard, but all too often the music is perceived by a good portion of the audience as an atmospheric accompaniment to a lavish dinner. This is especially shaming since many of the musicians currently performing have set new standards of technical excellence. David Murray and Arthur Blythe seem able to do everything on the tenor and alto saxophone, respectively; Charlie Haden and Fred Hopkins are among the greatest bassists of all time; Tony Williams and Jack DeJohnette are among the greatest drummers; John Hicks and William Henderson are superlative pianists. And yet, even given this standard of musical excellence, it is unlikely that jazz will ever again achieve the concentration of excitement that it did in the days of Parker or Coltrane. Coltrane's "sheets of sound" style remains massively influential and any number of young players can race their way through ten-minute Coltrane-like solos—but with little of the feeling that distinguishes both the master and his most distinguished disciples like Pharoah Sanders. Listening to them, you are tempted, even when impressed, to respond like Lester Young: "Yeah, man . . . but can you sing me a song?" Perhaps this is why a lot of attention is focused on bebop and its variants. However expertly played, modern versions of bebop lack the sense of discovery that animates every note of the music of Parker and Gillespie. Bebop has become formula music, a music whose syntax, in the face of what succeeded it, is as simple as that of a sentence like "The boy throws the ball through the window." In the 1940s no one had thrown balls through windows like that before and it was exciting to hear people do it over and over again. That action is no longer fascinating in itself. What still makes bebop interesting is how hard the ball is thrown, how many pieces the window shatters into. At their best today's bebop players leave you watching shards of glass dancing in the air, remembering the gorgeous arc made by the ball. In a slow number the ball will be tossed so gently that the glass shivers but remains intact.

·

The long shadow of Coltrane and the question of what can still be said in the bebop idiom are part of a larger doubt facing contemporary jazz players: does any new and important work remain to be done?[31] Although scarcely a century old the rapid evolution of jazz means that audience and performers alike share a sense of coming very late in the tradition. Whether, after Bloom, we call this "the anxiety of influence" or generalize it further into the postmodern condition hardly matters: the important thing is that jazz is now inescapably preoccupied with its own tradition. Indeed, art critic Robert Hughes's vision "of a present with continuous roots in history, where an artist's every action is judged by the unwearying tribunal of the dead," is as endemic to today's jazz musicians as it is (to Hughes's immense regret) inimical to contemporary visual artists.[32] Whereas the jazz of the radical 1960s was preoccupied with breaking from tradition, the neoclassical 1980s were concerned with affirming it. But this distinction is in danger of collapsing almost as soon as it is made. Since its tradition is one of innovation and improvisation, jazz, it could be argued, is never more traditional than when it is boldly iconoclastic. The art form most devoted to its past, jazz has always been the most forward-looking, so that the most radical work is often simultaneously the most traditional (Ornette Coleman's music, offered and perceived as nothing less than the Change of the Century, was drenched in the blues he had grown up hearing in Fort Worth). Either way, revivalism of any kind is doomed—it contradicts one of the animating principles of the music—but the development of jazz is now dependent on its capacity to absorb the past, and the most adventurous music is, increasingly, that which is

[31] Cf. Bloom, *The Anxiety of Influence*, p. 148.
[32] Robert Hughes. *Nothing If Not Critical* (New York: Alfred A. Knopf, 1990), p. 402.

able to dig deepest and most widely into the tradition. In this respect it is significant that, while in the past many musicians made their most important and innovative contributions when young, the most innovative players of our age are tending toward their forties. Jazz was still a youthful music when Bird and Diz revolutionized it; now jazz has entered its middle age and so have those who are its most telling representatives.

Lester Bowie and Henry Threadgill, for example. For years the Art Ensemble of Chicago—of which Bowie is a founder member—has proclaimed its commitment to "Great Black Music—Ancient to the Future," and Bowie's recent, less overtly experimental work with the Brass Fantasy is totally—if lightheartedly—in keeping with this rubric. Bowie's trumpet covers the whole history of the instrument from Armstrong onward; drawing on material from Billie Holiday to Sade, he delights as much in contemporary pop songs as he does in the expressive freedom afforded by his work with the Art Ensemble. The resulting pastiche somehow contrives to be both reverential and uproarious—Serious Fun, as he puts it—as he moves in the space of a note from muted emotion to chuckles, slurs, and howls. Again this is in keeping with the tradition: a good solo has other members of the band smiling, a great solo cracks them up.

Bowie's virtuoso performances take Louis Armstrong—the man who made jazz into a soloist's art—as their starting point; Threadgill reaches back even further, to pre-Armstrong New Orleans when the group sound was paramount. While a succession of solos usually achieves serial peaks of excitement, in Threadgill solos are no more privileged than duets, trios, or ensemble passages, the texture of sound shifting constantly between different permutations of the sextet's unusual instrumentation: drum and cello, cello and bass, drum and drum, drums and trumpet, trumpet and bass and cello. The complexity and density of his compositions are such that the resulting sound feels as indebted to the conservatoire avant-garde as to the jazz tradition.

If Threadgill and Bowie embody a certain relation to tradition—one shaped to a large extent by their mutual involvement in Chicago's AACM (the Association for the Advancement of Creative Musicians)—then another, equally powerful relation is personified by the Marsalis brothers, Wynton and Branford. From the 1950s onward jazz evolved at such a hectic pace that the possibilities of a given innovation were no sooner glimpsed than the music was hurrying on elsewhere. Hence there remains considerable potential in exploring ground that has ostensibly already been covered, and this is what Wynton and Branford have been doing. Wynton does not have a sound that is uniquely his own and, at least until *The Majesty of the Blues* (a more experimental venture), he was not breaking new ground formally, but was using the work—and sound—of Dizzy and Miles and taking it a stage further than they were able to, incorporating all sorts of technical possibilities (like the growls and slurs of Bowie) that have become available only since the heyday of bop. Technically Marsalis must be one of the best trumpeters ever and he is never less than exhilarating when performing live. While I do not share the common criticism of him that he is simply duplicating what has been done before, some doubts nevertheless creep in while listening to virtuosi like Marsalis and Jon Faddis (who takes Dizzy's work in the high range to what seems like its biological limit). Earlier I spoke of jazz evolving in such a way that in the process of answering questions it simultaneously raised new ones. Faddis and the Marsalis brothers are providing superbly articulate answers; they are not raising many questions.

A third tendency, related to but distinct from the two described above, can be seen in the work of musicians who came to prominence as "free" or "energy" players and who are now going back to more traditional forms. People like David Murray and Archie Shepp did not have to fight for musical freedom the way Coltrane did (Murray was twelve when Coltrane died); they inherited the wide expressive space of free jazz just as Coltrane inherited the bebop format. Now, as part of their musical *advancement*, Murray and Shepp have gone back to tighter forms, investing them with all the intensity of their free-blowing, energy years. Roland Kirk sardonically said that you couldn't appreciate freedom unless you'd been in prison. Much of the best jazz in recent years is less a relinquishing of freedom than a means of better appreciating it.

The best jazz of the late 1980s touched on aspects of all three of these overlapping relations to the past and no group better exemplified this than The Leaders, an all-star cooperative featuring Lester Bowie, Arthur Blythe, Chico Freeman, Don Moye, Kirk Lightsey, and Cecil McBee. If the whole of jazz history were rolled up into a ball and pressed into a record a sound very like that of The Leaders would probably result.

The integration of music across time has been accompanied by an equally powerful trend to integrate music across geography. Musicians in the 1960s increasingly incorporated explicit Eastern and African rhythms—and instruments—into their music. Latin and African jazz are now firmly established styles, but some of the most individual and inventive musical cross-fertilization still comes from those like Pharoah Sanders and Don Cherry who were among the first to draw inspiration from non-Western music (listen to the Oriental blues "Japan" on Sanders' 1967 album *Tauhid*). Cherry in particular seems able to retain an astonishing portion of the world's music in his ongoing creative development. Though he built his reputation on the free jazz scene as trumpeter in the Ornette Coleman Quartet he is proficient on any number of instruments and is equally at home in any setting from reggae to the ethnic folk music of Mali or Brazil. Probably the most impressive big band in the world, albeit one which is not in permanent existence, the Liberation Music Orchestra, led by Cherry's longtime associate, bassist Charlie Haden, draws on Spanish Civil War tunes and revolutionary anthems to create a music which, although pervaded by the improvisational spirit of the avant-garde, is still faithful to the spirit of its sources.

Some of the most impressive jazz is now found on the fringes of the form, where, in any kind of limiting sense, it is scarcely jazz at all. In the interstices of world music, jazz is apparent as a determining force in shifting multivalent compounds. A crucial album in this respect was *Grazing Dreams* featuring, inter alios, Collin Walcott, Jan Garbarek, and, naturally, Don Cherry. *Shakti*, featuring Indian violinist Shankar, Zakir Hussain on tabla, and John McLaughlin on guitar, offered further trailblazing prospects. In recent years the Beiruti oud player Rabih Abou-Khalil has produced half a dozen uncategorizable albums combining the traditions of jazz and Arabic music, featuring players like Charlie Mariano who, musically speaking, are at home anywhere in the world. (Special mention should also be made of the extraordinary recordings Mariano made with the singer R. A. Ramamani and the Karnataka College of Percussion.) Another top oud player, Anouar Brahem, from Tunisia, can be heard in drifting, meditative collaboration with Jan Garbarek on the remarkable *Madar*. This may well prove to be the most fruitful and creative area of exploration in the future.

Many of these encounters were recorded in Europe (in Germany particularly), which has often seemed more important in providing a receptive audience for American musicians than in forging talent of its own. In fact Britain—to narrow our focus for a moment—has produced dozens of influential musicians who can hold their own with the best players in the world (bassist Dave Holland, baritone saxophonist John Surman, guitarist John McLaughlin, and trumpeter Kenny Wheeler come immediately to mind). Within the UK, however, their achievement has scarcely been adequately recognized—indeed, it has, if anything, been eclipsed by a new generation of players. Saxophonists Courtney Pine, Andy Sheppard, Tommy Smith, and Steve Williamson, for example, have all made a strong impression on the contemporary scene but it is still too early to tell if they will make a lasting impact internationally—or indeed to tell if the current fascination for all things jazz will prove more than a fad.

The most significant contribution to the creation of music on the Continent, however, has probably been in the shape of record labels rather than performers (though this is not to diminish the importance of musicians like bassist Eberhard Weber, trombonist Albert Mangelsdorff, or saxophonist Jan Garbarek). Black Saint in Italy, Enja in Germany, and Steeplechase in Denmark have given considerable artistic license to a roster of first-class musicians whose work would not have been deemed viable by the increasingly corporate nature of the record industry in America. The most important European label, however, is undoubtedly Manfred Eicher's ECM (Editions of Contemporary Music). Like Blue Note in the 1950s and 1960s, ECM has evolved a sound so distinctive that it has actually come to denote a style of music—a style which, in spite of the number of American musicians in the catalogue, is felt to be distinctly European.[33] Although it is unfairly criticized as sometimes purveying a faintly more animated form of ambient music—it seems to be forgotten that some of the best work of the Art Ensemble and Jack DeJohnette is on ECM—the ECM sound is certainly moving toward a modernist chamber music with recordings of solo cello by Dave Holland, unaccompanied guitar by Ralph Towner, and, of course, the huge output of solo piano by Keith Jarrett. What is most interesting about ECM's music is that it is almost wholly unburdened by the weight of history, by the anxiety of influence, that dominates most other contemporary jazz; and no one exemplifies this more completely than Jarrett. Significantly, Jarrett is the most European of American jazz musicians, the most deeply indebted to Western classical music (he has recorded Bach's *Das Wohltemperierte Klavier* for ECM). Jarrett is as much the heir of Rilke (one of whose *Sonnets to Orpheus* is quoted on the sleeve of the magnificent—and, incidentally, utterly non-Western—*Spirits*) and Liszt as he is of Bill Evans or Bud Powell, and in much of his recent solo work it is only his unshakable commitment to rhythm and improvisation—rather than any attachment to blue notes—that keeps him in the jazz tradition. When Jarrett is at his best, snatches of all kinds of music float through his work but there is never any sense of strain,

[33] It should also be noted that ECM has long been committed to providing a context for encounters between Western and non-Western musicians and musical forms. See, for example, the outstanding albums featuring Shankar, Collin Walcott, Zakir Hussain, and Nana Vasconcelos.

of a conscious effort to combine these disparate influences. Rather, to adopt his own version of the process of creation, he makes his mind as blank as possible and the music seems simply to sweep through him. Our enjoyment of Threadgill and Bowie depends to an extent on our recognizing how different aspects of a common musical heritage are being combined. Our enjoyment of Jarrett, on the other hand, derives from the music coming together in such a way that, even when its origins are apparent, its *essence* lies so totally in Jarrett's improvisational genius as to seem impossible to account for: mysterious, timeless.

John Berger has written that "the moment at which a piece of music begins provides a clue to the nature of all art."[34] The suggestive force of Berger's formulation, "the incongruity of that moment, compared to the uncounted, unperceived silence which preceded it," is never more powerfully felt than when Jarrett's fingers touch the keys. Considerable though it may be, the sense of moment when Alfred Brendel prepares to play Schubert is less than when Jarrett prepares to improvise because, even if we have never heard the piece before, we know we are witnessing an act of *re*-creation rather than creation itself; we are, in other words, one stage removed from Steiner's republic of the primary. Extraordinarily, the sense of being witness to the moment of creation scarcely diminishes as Jarrett's music proceeds. In Jarrett the perpetual creation of the music means that the "moment" Berger refers to is contained in every second of the music's duration. This is why his music holds us so intimately within its own self-generating sense of time. Or rather, his music affects time as a snowfall affects sound: re-

[34] John Berger, "The Moment of Cubism," in *The White Bird* (London: Chatto/Tigerstripe, 1985), p. 186.

placing what was noticeable with an absence more strongly felt than what is normally so perceptibly present.[35]

6

Jarrett is exceptional and so is the experience of listening to him. In every other respect the contemporary listener is faced with a problem similar to that of the contemporary performer. When we put on a jazz album these days, to adapt Bloom again, "we listen to hear a distinctive voice, if we can, and if the voice is not already somewhat differentiated from its precursors and fellows, then we tend to stop listening, no matter what the voice is attempting to *say*."[36]

In the case of jazz this perhaps applies even more strongly to past masters than it does to contemporary players. Jorge Luis Borges has pointed out that *Ulysses* now seems to come—because we encounter it first—before *The Odyssey*, and in exactly the same way Miles comes before Armstrong, Coltrane before Hawkins. Typically, the person coming to jazz plunges in somewhere (*Kind of Blue* is a frequent starting point but for many it will, increasingly, be John Zorn or Courtney Pine) and then goes both forward and back. This is a

[35] The snow/silence comment suggests another point which has a relevance beyond Jarrett. Apart from a brief period with Miles Davis, Jarrett has been unwavering in his commitment to acoustic as opposed to electronic instruments. Electronic instruments define themselves in relation to—and partake of the quality of—din. Acoustic instruments define themselves in relation to—and partake of the quality of—silence. For this reason acoustic instruments will always have a greater purity. The title track of Charlie Haden's album *Silence* (with Chet Baker, Enrico Pieranunzi, and Billy Higgins) is a beautiful and fragile demonstration of precisely this point.

[36] Bloom, *The Anxiety of Influence*, p. 148.

shame since jazz is best appreciated chronologically
(Parker seems less startling when we come to him via
the screams of Pharoah Sanders). More generally,
even if we have never actually heard their records, we
hear Louis Armstrong, Lester Young, Coleman Hawkins, Art Tatum, and Bud Powell in almost every piece
of jazz we come across. When we do get around to
listening to Bud Powell it is difficult to see what is so
special about him: he sounds like any other pianist
(though really what we mean is that every other pianist
sounds like Bud Powell). The positive side of this relation to the past is that moving deeper into the tradition can be as much a voyage of discovery as moving
forward through it: instead of following the river to its
mouth we trace it to its source. As you move further
back, so you are able to recognize the special traits of
the predecessors; it is like seeing a photo of your great-
grandfather and recognizing the origins of your grand-
children's features in his face.

The ongoing influence of the tradition ensures that
past masters are present throughout the music's evolution and development. Old recordings, meanwhile,
are digitally remastered and repackaged to make them
sound and look like new; and some of the newest-
sounding music is that which is most saturated in the
past. Ideas of forward and backward, the sense of past
and present, of old and new dreams, begin to dissolve
into each other in the twilight of perpetual noon.

Sources

Select Discography

Acknowledgments

Sources

Most of the quotations from musicians are duplicated in any number of books about jazz. I have not mentioned articles from which I used just one quotation or detail in the whole book. Throughout I relied more on photographs than on written sources, especially on the work of Carol Reiff, William Claxton, Christer Landergren, Milt Hinton, Herman Leonard, William Gottlieb, Bob Parent, and Charles Stewart.

LESTER YOUNG: Transcripts from court-martial; John McDonough, "The Court-Martial of Lester Young," *Downbeat*, January 1981, p. 18; Robert Reisner's article in *Downbeat*, April 30, 1959. The biggest help was Dennis Stock's justly famous photograph of Lester in the Alvin Hotel.

THELONIOUS MONK: Nat Hentoff's illuminating piece in *The Jazz Life* (New York: Dial Press, 1961); Joe Goldberg's piece in *Jazz Masters of the 50s* (New York: Macmillan, 1965); Val Wilmer's piece in *Jazz People* (London: Allison & Busby, 1970). The text incorporates remarks of Monk's reported by Steve Lacy, Charlie Rouse, and others. My most fertile source was Charlotte Zwerin's excellent compilation of archive footage, *Thelonious Monk: Straight No Chaser*—for my money the best film about a jazz musician I have ever seen.

BUD POWELL: For the episode at Birdland: Ross Russell's evocative *Bird Lives* (London: Quartet, 1973); also *Miles: The Autobiography* by Miles Davis with Quincy Troupe (New York: Simon & Schuster, 1989). The remark about "The Glass Enclosure" was derived from Nietzsche's description of Beethoven's sonata no. 29 in B flat, op. 106, "Hammerklavier," in *Human, All Too Human* (Cambridge: Cambridge University Press, 1986), p. 91. Some of the best photographs of Bud Powell were taken by Dennis Stock but—ironically, since this chapter relies so heavily on photographs—I did not come across them until the manuscript was complete.

CHARLES MINGUS: Bill Whitworth's piece in *New York Herald Tribune*, November 1, 1964; Brian Priestley's thorough *Mingus: A Critical Biography* (New York: Da Capo, 1984); Mingus' autobiography, *Beneath the Underdog* (New York: Alfred A. Knopf, 1971); Janet Coleman and Al Young's memoir, *Mingus/Mingus* (Berkeley: Creative Art Books, 1989).

BEN WEBSTER: John Jeremy's documentary *The Brute and the Beautiful*; Nat Shapiro and Nat Hentoff, *Hear Me Talkin' to Ya* (New York: Dover Press. 1955).

CHET BAKER: My sources were either apocryphal or visual: hundreds of photographs and Bruce Weber's documentary *Let's Get Lost*.

ART PEPPER: My most useful source was the autobiography, *Straight Life* (New York: Schirmer, 1979). Co-written with his wife, Laurie, it is indispensable for an understanding of Pepper and riveting reading for anyone interested in jazz. The first, fourth, and fifth parts of this section are based on episodes mentioned briefly in that book. I also drew on Don McGlynn's excellent documentary *Art Pepper: Notes of a Jazz Survivor*.

DUKE ELLINGTON AND HARRY CARNEY: Derek Jewell, *Duke: A Portrait of Duke Ellington* (New York: Norton, 1980); Stanley Dance, *The World of Duke Ellington* (New York: Scribner's, 1970); James Lincoln Collier, *Duke Ellington* (New York: Oxford University Press, 1987); Whitney Balliett's piece in *Ecstasy at the Onion* (New York: Oxford University Press, 1971); Duke

Ellington, *Music Is My Mistress* (New York: Doubleday, 1973); Mercer Ellington with Stanley Dance, *Duke Ellington in Person* (Boston: Houghton Mifflin, 1978).

The comments about Pepper's weakness and Baker's tenderness were suggested by Adorno's remarks about Verlaine and the young Brahms, respectively, in *Aesthetic Theory* (London: Routledge & Kegan Paul, 1984). Adorno's essay "Perennial Fashion: Jazz," in *Prisms*, incidentally, is a very silly piece of work indeed.

On the hunt for information my first stop was always *Jazz: The Essential Companion* by Ian Carr, Digby Fairweather, and Brian Priestley (London: Grafton, 1987), not as informative as the rather arid *New Grove Dictionary of Jazz* edited by Barry Kernfeld (New York: Grove's Dictionaries of Music, 1988), but to my mind rather more enjoyable.

Select Discography

A

Only albums recorded as leader are included

LESTER YOUNG: *The Lester Young Story* (CBS); *Pres in Europe* (Onyx); *Lester Leaps Again* (Affinity); *Live in Washington D.C.* (Pablo). Lester Young and Coleman Hawkins: *Classic Tenors* (CBS).

THELONIOUS MONK: *Genius of Modern Music Vols. 1 and 2* (Blue Note); *Alone in San Francisco*; *Brilliant Corners*; *With John Coltrane*; *Monk's Music*; *Misterioso* (Riverside); *The Composer*; *Underground*; *Monk's Dream* (Atlantic); *The Complete Black Lion/ Vogue Recordings* (Mosaic Box Set).

BUD POWELL: *The Amazing Bud Powell Vols. 1 and 2*; *The Scene Changes*; *Time Waits* (Blue Note); *The Genius of Bud Powell*; *Jazz Giant* (Verve); *Time Was* (RCA).

BEN WEBSTER: *No Fool, No Fun*; *Makin' Whoopee* (Spotlite); *Coleman Hawkins Encounters Ben Webster*; *King of the Tenors* (Verve); *See You at the Fair* (Impulse); *At Work in Europe* (Prestige); *Ben Webster Plays Ballads*; *Ben Webster Plays Ellington* (Storyville); *Live at Pio's* (Enja); *Live in Amsterdam* (Affinity).

CHARLES MINGUS: *Blues and Roots*; *The Clown*; *Live at Antibes*; *Oh Yeah*; *Pithecanthropus Erectus*; *Three or Four Shades of Blues* (Atlantic); *Tijuana Moods* (RCA); *The Black Saint and the Sinner Lady*; *Charles Mingus Plays Piano* (Impulse); *Ah-Um* (CBS); *At Monterey*; *Portrait* (Prestige); *Abstractions*; *New York Sketchbook*

(Affinity); *Complete Candid Recordings* (Mosaic Box Set); *In Europe Vols. 1 and 2* (Enja); *Live in Châteauvallon; Meditation* (INA).

CHET BAKER: *Chet; In New York; Once Upon a Summertime* (Riverside); *Complete Pacific—Live and Studio—Jazz Recordings with Russ Freeman* (Mosaic Box Set); *Chet Baker and Crew* (Pacific); *When Sunny Gets Blue* (Steeplechase); *Peace* (Enja). Chet Baker and Art Pepper: *Playboys* (Pacific).

ART PEPPER: *Live at the Village Vanguard (Thursday, Friday and Saturday); Living Legend; Art Pepper Meets the Rhythm Section; No Limit; Smack Up; The Trip* (Contemporary); *Today; Winter Moon* (Galaxy); *Modern Art; The Return of Art Pepper* (Blue Note); *Blues for the Fisherman* (Mole—released as Milcho Leviev Quartet).

B
Tradition, Influence, and Innovation

RABIH ABOU-KHALIL: *Al-Jadida; Blue Camel; Tarab; The Sultan's Picnic* (Enja).

ART ENSEMBLE OF CHICAGO: *Nice Guys; Full Force* (includes "Charlie M"); *Urban Bushmen* (ECM); *Message to Our Folks* (Affinity); *Naked* (DIW).

ALBERT AYLER: *Love Cry* (Impulse); *Vibrations* (with Don Cherry) (Freedom).

LESTER BOWIE'S BRASS FANTASY: *The Great Pretender; Avant-Pop, I Only Have Eyes for You* (ECM); *Serious Fun* (DIW).

DON CHERRY: *Brown Rice; Multikulti* (A & M); *El Corazón* (with Ed Blackwell) (ECM); *Codona; Codona 2; Codona 3* (with Nana Vasconcelos and Collin Walcott) (ECM).

ORNETTE COLEMAN: *The Shape of Jazz to Come; Change of the Century; Free Jazz* (with Don Cherry, Charlie Haden, and Ed Blackwell) (Atlantic).

JOHN COLTRANE: *Giant Steps; The Avant-Garde* (with Don Cherry); *My Favorite Things; Olé* (Atlantic); *Africa/Brass; Live at the Village Vanguard; Impressions; Coltrane; Duke Ellington and John Coltrane* (includes "Take the Coltrane"); *A Love Supreme;*

First Meditations (for Quartet); Ascension; Sun Ship; Meditations; Live in Seattle; Live at the Village Vanguard Again!; Live in Japan Vols. 1 and 2 (includes "Peace on Earth") (Impulse).

MILES DAVIS: Round about Midnight; Milestones; Kind of Blue; Sketches of Spain (Columbia).

JACK DEJOHNETTE: Special Edition (with Arthur Blythe and David Murray); New Directions; New Directions in Europe (both with Lester Bowie) (ECM).

JOHNNY DYANI: Song for Biko (with Don Cherry); Witchdoctor's Son (Steeplechase).

DUKE ELLINGTON: Black, Brown and Beige (RCA); Duke Ellington Meets Coleman Hawkins (Impulse); Money Jungle (with Max Roach and Charles Mingus) (Blue Note).

JON FADDIS: Into the Faddisphere (Epic).

JAN GARBAREK: Madar (with Anouar Brahem and Shaukat Hussain) (ECM).

CHARLIE HADEN: Silence (with Chet Baker) (Soul Note); Charlie Haden and the Liberation Music Orchestra (Impulse); Ballad of the Fallen (ECM); Dream Keeper (Blue Note).

ZAKIR HUSSAIN: Making Music (with John McLaughlin, Haraprasad Chaurasia, and Jan Garbarek) (ECM).

KEITH JARRETT: Facing You; Köln Concert; Sun Bear Concerts; Concerts; Paris Concert; Spirits (solo); Vienna Concert; Paris Concert; Eyes of the Heart; The Survivors Suite (with Charlie Haden, Paul Motian, and Dewey Redman); Belonging; My Song; Personal Mountains (with Jan Garbarek, Palle Danielsson, and Jon Christensen); Changeless; The Cure; Bye Bye Blackbird (with Jack DeJohnette and Gary Peacock) (ECM).

THE LEADERS: Mudfoot (Black Hawk); Out Here Like This; Unforeseen Blessings (Black Saint).

CHARLIE MARIANO and the Karnataka College of Percussion featuring R. A. Ramamani: Jyothi (ECM); Live (Verabra).

JOHN MCLAUGHLIN: Shakti (with Shankar and Zakir Hussain) (CBS).

WYNTON MARSALIS: Live at the Blues Alley; The Majesty of the Blues (CBS).

DAVID MURRAY: *Flowers for Albert; Live at the Lower Manhattan Ocean Club* (with Lester Bowie) (India Navigation); *Ming; Murray's Steps; Home; The Hill* (Black Saint); *Ming's Samba* (CBS).

OLD AND NEW DREAMS: (Don Cherry, Charlie Haden, Ed Blackwell, Dewey Redman): first album (Black Saint); second album and *Playing* (ECM).

SONNY ROLLINS: *All the Things You Are* (with Coleman Hawkins) (Blue Bird); *East Broadway Run Down* (with McCoy Tyner, Jimmy Garrison, and Elvin Jones) (Impulse); *Tenor Madness* (with John Coltrane) (Prestige).

PHAROAH SANDERS: *Karma; Tauhid* (includes "Japan") (Impulse); *A Prayer Before Dawn* (includes "Living Space"); *Journey to the One; Heart Is a Melody; Live* (Theresa); *Moonchild* (Timeless).

SHANKAR: *Song for Everyone* (with Jan Garbarek, Zakir Hussain, Trilok Gurtu) (ECM). (See also John McLaughlin.)

ARCHIE SHEPP: *Fire Music* (Impulse); *Goin' Home* (with Horace Parlan) (Steeplechase); *Steam; Soul Song* (Enja).

HENRY THREADGILL: *Easily Slip into Another World; Rag, Bush and All; You Know the Number* (Novus).

COLLIN WALCOTT: *Grazing Dreams* (with Palle Daniellson, John Abercrombie, Dom Um Romao, Don Cherry) (ECM). (See also the *Codona* albums with Cherry and Nana Vasconcelos.)

Acknowledgments

I am indebted to: Horst Liepolt at Sweet Basil's, Dan Melnick at the Blue Note, Michael Dorf at the Knitting Factory, and Raphael at Carlos I; Terri Hinte at Fantasy, Didier Deutsch at Atlantic, Milhan Gorkey at Blue Note, Theresa Brilli at CBS, Renee Foster and Michael Reading at MCA, Marilyn Lipsius at BMG, Bob Cummins at India Navigation, Allen Pitman at Theresa, Charlie Lourie at Mosaic, Mike Wilpizeski at Polygram, Barney Fields at Savoy, Francois Zalacain at Sunnyside, Giovanni Bonandrini at Black Saint, and the press officers at Enja, ECM, and Storyville.

Thanks also: to Xandra Hardie, Frances Coady, and Pascal Cariss; to Ian Carr for reading the manuscript and making several useful suggestions, to Chris Mitchell for his guidance and close scrutiny of the Afterword, to Charles De Ledesma for his musical enthusiasm.

Slowly Tommy looked at the very large grown-up standing in the doorway. He wore a sleek silver workout suit, which fit snugly across his wide shoulders. His hair was blond and shiny, gelled and combed back so perfectly, the rake marks were still visible. He carried a clipboard and had a pen behind one ear. Around his neck was a shiny chain, and in his mouth was a silver whistle, which he had just blown. His steely blue eyes panned across the sea of babies.

"I gots a bad feeling about this, Tommy," muttered Chuckie, eyeing the man's cross-trainers. "A really bad feeling."

Rugrats Chapter Books

Just Wanna HAVE FUN

ISBN 0-439-16498-2

12 11 10 9 8 7 6 5 4 3 2 1   0 1 2 3 4 5/0

Printed in the U.S.A.

First Scholastic printing, May 2000

Just Wanna HAVE FUN

by Sarah Willson
illustrated by Gary Fields

SCHOLASTIC INC.

New York   Toronto   London   Auckland   Sydney
Mexico City   New Delhi   Hong Kong

Chapter 1

Stu Pickles sighed contentedly and took a sip of his frothy pink drink. He plucked out the little green umbrella from his glass and twirled it between his fingers.

"This sure is a great place, Deed," he said, gazing around the pool area of the Sliver of Sand Resort. Two feeble palm trees swayed on the concrete deck.

"It's just like the brochure promised—

a relaxing family vacation, all-day buffets, pool and spa, and best of all, coordinated events for the kids to do all day long while we relax. And two whole weeks of it! Who cares if the place isn't *right* on the beach? We can definitely glimpse it from here if we stand on the table."

"I think it's terrific too, Stu," Didi replied. She was lying on a lounge chair, reading a thick book entitled *Your Child, Your Fault.*

"The Relaxation and Stress-Relief Techniques classes are wonderful!" Didi continued. "The instructor is world-famous!" Then she frowned thoughtfully. "Do you think Tommy and Dil are enjoying it as much as we are?"

"Oh, sure, honey," Stu replied. "They've got that nice events coordinator, Cindy, organizing all their activities, and

that impressive-looking Swedish guy, Carlssen, running the Babycize program. They're having a blast!"

"Well, the staff do seem enthusiastic," said Didi, turning another page. "I just love the costumes the waiters wear at the kids' mealtimes; I'm sure the kids love them too."

Chuckie's dad, Chas, came striding up from the beach. He wore a sun visor and carried a half-pound dumbbell in each hand. "Hi, guys!" he panted.

"My, you weren't gone very long," said Didi.

"Well, this stretch of beach is kind of short," Chas said. "The beach ends after about ten feet, and then becomes slippery boulders. But this place is still great! Look at this pool area with pool-side service and everything!"

A waiter dressed as Tarzan staggered

over with a huge bowl of tropical fruit, which he placed on a nearby table.

Chas set down his weights and strolled over to pick up an enormous coconut. He studied it for a moment, then set it down and reached for a pineapple.

"Ow!" he said as he pricked his finger on the fruit. Chas sucked on his finger before asking, "Uh, anyone for a game of Nerf Ping-Pong in the game room?"

Didi glanced at her watch. Suddenly she clapped shut her book and jumped up. "I have to find Betty! It's almost time for our Relaxation and Stress-Relief Techniques class. I wonder where she is? The instructor gets so upset when anyone walks in late."

Just then Phil and Lil's mother, Betty, trotted out from the spa area.

"Sorry, Deed," she said. "Howard just

had a pH-balanced, rain-forest mud treatment, and he let it dry too long. Had to crack him open with a croquet mallet!"

"Oh, dear, I hope he's all right," Didi said. "We just have time to peek in on the kids on our way. Do you think they're enjoying this vacation as much as we are?"

"Why wouldn't they?" asked Betty.

Chapter 2

"I don't like this bacation one bit, Tommy," whispered Chuckie. They were sitting on an exercise mat, along with their friends Phil and Lil, and Tommy's baby brother, Dil. About ten other babies sat with them. "This morning the Big Bad Wolf gave me oatmeal! I got so scareded, I couldn't eat it!"

"Don't worry, Chuckie," replied Tommy. "We're just here to have fun.

And that growed-up, Cindy, is nice."

They both looked over at the perky and suntanned events coordinator, who was squeaking excitedly on a cell phone while pulling a long pink strand of gum from her mouth and twisting it around her finger.

"Yeah," agreed Phil. "She lets us do anything we want. She didn't even yell when Lil ate some green finger paint."

"Or when Phil drew a picture on the wall with a marker," chimed in Lil.

PHTWEEEEEEEEEEEEET!

All the babies in the room jumped at the shrill sound of a whistle. Even Tommy's baby brother, Dil, stopped shaking his rattle and looked up from his baby bouncy seat.

The door to the exercise room suddenly opened. A long shadow fell over the babies. Slowly Tommy looked at the very large grown-up standing in the doorway. He wore a sleek silver workout suit, which fit snugly across his wide shoulders. His hair was blond and shiny, gelled and combed back so perfectly, the rake marks were still visible. He carried a clipboard and had a pen behind one ear. Around his neck was a shiny chain, and in his mouth was a silver whistle, which he had just blown. His steely blue eyes panned across the sea of babies.

The babies stopped fidgeting and looked expectantly at him.

"I gots a bad feeling about this, Tommy," muttered Chuckie, eyeing the man's cross-trainers. "A really bad feeling."

Cindy hurriedly clicked off her phone and spoke to them.

"Kids, this *very* nice man is Mr. Carlssen, the head of the Babycize program. He'll be working with *all* of you for the next two weeks."

Cindy examined her pearly pink nails as she spoke. "We are *so* lucky to *have* him!" She gestured wanly toward Mr. Carlssen, then patted her perfect ponytail.

The babies stared up at him. The room was silent, except for the sound of Dil sucking on his Binky.

Mr. Carlssen bared his front teeth at Cindy, as though it were a great effort to smile. Then he began pacing slowly back and forth in front of the babies, his hands clasped across the clipboard on his broad chest.

"I am indeed Mr. Carlssen," he began. "I yust love to work with cheeldren. I have trained many, many babies to grow up to become excellent athletes. There is *no* reason at all . . ." he said,

"that I cannot train you, too."

He looked around. His gaze rested on Chuckie's black socks before he added, "Your parents want to take home winners—*and only winners*. It is my yob to make sure that they do! *So*."

Just then Dil picked up a sippy cup and lobbed it at the far wall. Its top flew off, and red juice spilled everywhere. The babies gasped.

Mr. Carlssen frowned at the mess, then he shrugged as he continued. "Next week you will all compete in the Sliver of Sand Resort's Baby Olympics!"

"Baby Limpings?" whispered Chuckie. "Why are we gonna be limping, Tommy?"

"Why does that guy talk funny?" asked Lil.

"How come he's wearing big baby shoes?" Phil wanted to know.

18

PHTWEEEEEEEEEEEEET!

Everyone was silent again. Mr Carlssen stared at them for what seemed like a long time.

"We will start with weight lifting," he finally said, "then move on to cardio-wascular." He nodded to Cindy, who started passing out tiny pink plastic dumbbells.

"Remember," said Mr. Carlssen. "I am here to teach you that *winning is everything.*"

Chapter 3

"Hi," panted a big baby. "I'm Baby Bobby Bubbles, but you can just call me Bubba."

"Hi," Tommy panted back. "I'm Tommy, and that's my friend Chuckie." Tommy was working on aerobic conditioning for the Wee Li'l Walker event. He was jumping up and down on a minitrampoline.

Chuckie and Bubba were next to him, sitting side by side in a toy rowboat,

pulling and pushing heavy wooden oars. Every few minutes Mr. Carlssen came by, stood in front of them with a huge bullhorn, and bellowed, "STROKE!"

"What're you here for?" asked Bubba.

"'Laxing Family Bacation," Tommy replied. "What about you?"

"'Laxing Monthlong Getaway. Me and my friend Victor over there have been here for days and days already. Our moms and dads were here on their humming-moon, and they wanted to come back with us kids."

"You guys look like you've been doing this for a long time," said Chuckie. He looked over at Victor, a large-sized baby who was running repeatedly toward a huge, padded blocking sled, driving his shoulder into it and whooping loudly.

"Yep. I'm undy-beated in the Wee Li'l Walker and the Tot Trot. Victor is the return champing in the Crib Climb."

"The Crib Climb?" repeated Chuckie.

"Mmm-hmm. Victor also plays violin, and he's a champing chess player too. And see the twins over there?" Bubba pointed toward a boy and a girl about the same age as Phil and Lil. "They are Edie and Petey—basketball players. You should see Edie's baby hook shot. Sweeeeet."

Chuckie stopped pulling. He glanced over at Edie and Petey, who were playing basketball at a baby-sized plastic hoop with Phil and Lil.

"But this is just for fun, right?" Chuckie asked worriedly. "We're here to play while the growed-ups exercise and eat a lot and stuff, right?"

Before Tommy or Bubba could reply, Mr. Carlssen noticed that Chuckie had stopped rowing. He trotted up to

Chuckie with the bullhorn.

"STROKE!"

Chuckie gulped and resumed rowing. Mr. Carlssen continued patrolling around the other exercising babies.

"Play? No way," muttered Bubba, pulling hard on his oar. "You heard what Mr. Carlssen said. If we don't win the Limpings, our parents won't want to take us home."

"They'd leave us here . . . forever?" asked Chuckie.

"Think so," Bubba replied.

Meanwhile Stu, Didi, Betty, Howard, and Chas were passing the baby exercise room on their way to the luncheon buffet. They peeked in.

"Awwwww," said Stu. "Aren't they cute, playing like they're doing real grown-up exercise?"

Didi smiled. "Look, even Dil is trying!"

She pointed at Dil, who was trying to pull himself up on a little play gym rigged with a special pull-up bar. Next to him a baby boy and a baby girl were pulling themselves up easily.

"Hey, check out our pups playing like they're shooting hoops!" bellowed Betty as she nudged Howard. She pointed at Phil and Lil. "And they're playing with another set of twins! How 'bout that!"

"Ooof!" Howard winced. "Do you think the instructors should be allowing those two kids to back into the basket like that?" He watched them a bit more, then cried out, "Look! That boy just stepped on Phil's toes! And that girl just threw an elbow into Lil!" He was just about to turn away when he spotted another move. "Those other twins just executed a perfect give-and-go," he added glumly.

"Aw, pshaw. It'll toughen up our tykes," said Betty.

Soon an athletic-looking couple wearing matching warm-up suits jogged up to them. "We're Donald and Donna Donovan," the man said to Stu, Didi, Betty, Howard, and Chas as he continued to jog in place. They peeked into the exercise room.

"Those are our twins—Edie and Petey," Donald said, beaming. "Donna started doing dribbling drills when she was four months pregnant so the babies would get used to the sound of the ball. I was showing 'em motion-offense videos before they could even sit up!"

Donna blushed. "Come on, honey," she said. "We have just enough time for three sets of lower-ab crunches before lunch. And I heard they're serving your favorite today: Sliver of Sand's Sliver of

Liver Sandwiches!" They jogged away.

Betty frowned and called out to Phil and Lil, "Philip! Follow through on your shot! Lillian! Get those hands in the passing lane!"

"Let's go. We probably shouldn't be interrupting," said Didi. "They look like they're having so much fun!"

She ushered the rest of the parents toward the dining room.

Chapter 4

Stu, Didi, Chas, Betty, and Howard took their seats at a large table with a few other grown-ups.

Stu picked up the flyer by his plate. "The Baby Olympics?" he read. "Looks like that Carlssen fellow is going to run it. He's planning a whole bunch of little kiddie events!"

"Oh, isn't that sweet!" said Didi. Then she wondered out loud, "Do you think we should really encourage them to participate in competitive sports like this at such a young age? It could damage their inner psyches and upset the equilibrium in their sense of self."

"Aw, Deed, it's just for fun," said Stu. "Look at this: They're even having events for the littlest ones." He chuckled. "Dil is competing in the Rattle Chuck against two other babies his age—Brittanica and Gordon."

"Brittanica is my little girl!" called a statuesque woman from down the table. "She has a wonderful arm!"

A large man two chairs down the table leaned over and clapped Stu on the back. Stu started coughing. "Name's Bubbles!" the man said loudly. "My boy Bubba is in the baby group too! You should see him on the trampoline! Kid's got a vertical leap, he does!"

Stu smiled tightly back at him. "Yeah? My boy Tommy is slated for the Wee Li'l Walker event. He's got some speed . . . I think."

"No kidding?" Bubbles hollered back. "My Bubba's in that event too. He's the returning champ. They have to build a big tower of blocks, then run at each other's tower with a baby walker to knock it down. He's also running the Tot Trot."

Chas cleared his throat. "I understand that my Chuckie is participating in that event," he volunteered.

Bubbles looked Chas up and down with some amusement. "Kid inherit his athletic ability from his dad, did he?" he guffawed.

Chas frowned and sat up straighter in his chair.

A woman across the table smiled

gaily at them. "My boy Victor just *loves* these organized events!" she said. "We've encouraged his talents in violin and chess. Who knew he was such a little athlete as well!"

Then she pointed toward Stu. "I think Victor's going to be competing in the Crib Climb against your little one! My husband is back in our room right now, mixing wheat germ into Victor's baby food!"

A man who was built like a minivan grinned heartily at the group. He thrust a catcher's mitt-sized hand toward Howard. "Name's Klondike. Defensive end, Notre Dame 'eighty-two."

Howard made a face as he pulled back his throbbing hand and quickly plunged it into his glass of ice water.

"My boy Walter is so far off the charts in height and weight, the doc had to

tape an extra sheet of graph paper to his chart!" Klondike laughed heartily as he helped himself to another leg of lamb.

After a respectful silence, Howard picked up the program and continued reading. "Look here! They've got an Iron Babe event!" he exclaimed. "The kids are supposed to crawl fifty feet, ride a push toy once around the track, then dash through a sprinkler!" He stopped reading and looked up. "Chuckie?" he wondered. "Nah. Phil? Nah."

"There's even a stroller race for parents to do with their kids!" said Betty.

Klondike stopped chewing for a moment. "I'm in that one wif Walfer and we're *defumately* gumma win!" he said as he slammed his hand on the table to show how sure he was.

"Right-ho," said Chas, picking up some of the flatware from the floor.

Suddenly the room was very quiet. The grown-ups all looked at one another with new eyes.

"We have work to do!" Stu told Didi.

"I haven't iced Brittanica's arm today," muttered Brittanica's mother.

Didi looked at Betty. "Should we postpone the Relaxation and Stress-Relief Techniques class?" she asked.

"You BETCHA!" replied Betty.

Everyone at the table pushed back their chairs and hurried off.

Chapter 5

The next day the babies were having lunch in the kids' dining room. The waiters and waitresses were again dressed in costumes.

"More cottage cheese, honey?" Little Miss Muffet asked Tommy. He put down his spoon and clamped his mouth shut.

"How about some more shepherd's pie?" Little Bo-peep said to Walter.

He gave a delighted squeal, and Bo-peep spooned another helping into his bowl.

Dil was in his high chair. He flung his rattle with all his might. It sailed through the air, making a perfect arc. It flew through the doorway, right into the dining room next door, where all the parents were being served a flaming platter of bright orange food. The rattle whizzed by Stu's ear.

"Huh?" said Stu. He looked at the rattle on the floor, then craned his neck to call out to Dil. "Atta boy, Dil!"

"Mommy is so proud of you, Dilly!" cooed Didi as she waved to him. "He threw his rattle the farthest today!" She beamed at the other parents.

Brittanica's mother cleared her throat. "Actually, my little girl's throw would have been the farthest had it not deflected off the head of the events coordinator, who was in her way."

Didi smiled coolly at her, then turned and waved at Dil again.

Meanwhile, back in the babies' dining room, the Big Bad Wolf approached Chuckie carrying a tray of crackers. Quick as lightning, Chuckie was out of his booster seat, streaking through the grown-ups' dining room, and headed outside.

Stu and Chas stared at Chuckie, astonished. Stu had been working out complicated mathematical equations on his cocktail napkin. He turned to Chas, eyebrows raised.

"Kid's got wheels," said Stu.

"Mmm-hmm," agreed Chas.

Stu opened up a small notebook and scanned a page. "Aunt Miriam's got him at sixteen to one in the Tot Trot. He's our dark horse. Smart money's on Chuckie."

"To think—*my* Chuckie!" said Chas proudly.

Stu leaned toward Chas. "Chas, you and Chuckie should represent us in the Stroller Run," he whispered.

Chas began coughing on his pu-pu platter. "B-B-But why me?" he asked, after he had recovered.

"Chuckie must have gotten his speed from his parents," said Stu, "so there's a fifty-fifty chance it came from you!" He motioned to a passing waiter, who was dressed as a gorilla. "Uh, cancel his butterscotch sundae. He'll have a wheat-grass milk shake instead," said Stu.

Chas made a face, but Stu simply added, "We'll have you take a nice, easy, five-mile warm-up run after lunch. Then we'll hit the weight room."

Chapter 6

"YUST DO IT!" Mr. Carlssen boomed at the babies. The babies were pushing baby walkers in all directions.

"Tomorrow the Olympics begin!" Mr. Carlssen called out. "I've cancelled all other activities! Your parents will be there to watch you. They will want you to succeed at *all* costs, to *win* at *any* price!"

"Your moms and dads will be so

proud!" Cindy chimed in as she checked herself out in the mirror.

"Proud?" echoed Phil to the babies. "They'll only be proud if we win our games. If we lose, our parents won't want to take us home with them."

Tommy looked at his little brother, who was chewing on a tiny dumbbell. "I sure hope Dil can win that Rattle Chuck event," he said grimly.

"Well, if Brittanica wins, you can take home a little sister instead!" said Lil brightly. "Your parents only want to take home a winner, so maybe she'll be the one!"

Tommy shook his head. "No, my mommy and daddy like Dil bestest," he said.

"But what will happen if I lose in the Wee Li'l Walker event? Maybe they'll take Bubba home instead of me.

I heard Mr. Snarlssen say Bubba was going to be a great yumper."

"What's a yumper, Tommy?" asked Chuckie, who had just joined them after trying to tumble on the mats nearby.

"I dunno," said Tommy, "but it probably looks like Bubba."

"Let's go work on our yump shots, Lillian," said Phil. "Edie and Petey have been playing with the basketball set all morning."

"Okay, Philip," said Lil.

Meanwhile, back in the swimming pool area, the parents were gearing up for the next day too.

Stu had just hung up with Aunt Miriam. "She wants a fiver on Bubba in the Wee Li'l Walker event," he said to Didi.

"She's betting against her own great-nephew?" cried Didi.

"Well, she wants Tommy for the Crib Climb, even though Victor's got five-to-one odds," Stu explained.

Chas was jogging on the treadmill while pushing a simulated stroller.

Betty was timing him with a stopwatch.

Howard was pouring sports drinks into the babies' training cups.

Victor's mother walked in. "It's time for his power nap," she told the other parents.

"We made a motivational tape for him to listen to while he sleeps. It encourages him to relax on the straightaways and lean into the curves." She hurried out.

Klondike lumbered past as he pushed Walter in the stroller. Walter was sitting on top of three huge concrete blocks.

"See ya at the starting line, Spinster!"

45

Klondike puffed at Chas.

Bubbles strode in and said, "I almost forgot to order Bubba's special training meal—minced steak and mashed potatoes!" He dashed off toward the kitchen.

Chapter 7

The big day finally arrived. Mr. Carlssen had a crazed look in his eyes. His usually perfect hair was mussed up. He strode around, muttering to himself. A few parents paced nervously back and forth. Some laced up booties, others gave their babies rubdowns.

Stu walked over and put his arm around Tommy. "Son," he said. "No matter what happens today, remember these words of advice."

He scratched his head. "Right. Uhh. Remember: Winning isn't everything, but it wouldn't hurt. Make your mom and dad proud! Make your little brother look up to you! Win one for the li'l sipper!" He smiled and patted Tommy's head.

PHTWEEEEEEEEEEET!

Mr. Carlssen blew the whistle. "Line up for the Stroller Run!" he boomed.

Stu, Didi, Betty, and Howard hurried over to the starting line to encourage Chas. Chuckie sat in the stroller, snugly strapped in and wearing a sturdy helmet.

Alongside them were three other pairs of contestants, including Mr. Klondike and Walter. Mr. Carlssen raised the starting gun. "On your mark . . . Yet set . . ."

BANG!

The strollers and parents were off—except for Chas and Chuckie.

"What's wrong, Chas?" yelled Stu.

"Stroller . . . won't . . . go . . ." panted Chas, straining to push Chuckie's stroller. They watched Walter and Klondike streak across the finish line.

The winners ran a victory lap around the pool area. Cindy handed them a huge pineapple tied with a bright blue ribbon.

Klondike acted like he had just scored a touchdown and threw the pineapple on the ground. The fruit burst into several hundred pieces.

Stu looked down at the back wheel of Chuckie's stroller.

"Something's wedged in here," he muttered. He plucked a small object out of the axle and held it up.

"A Binky?" said Didi.

"A Binky," replied Stu darkly.

"Sabotage," gasped Howard.

"Surely somebody must have dropped it in there by accident," said Chas, mopping his brow.

"Maybe," replied Stu. "But, then again, maybe *not*! This," he muttered, "means war."

"Next event is the Rattle Chuck!" called Mr. Carlssen. Everyone hurried over to where Dil, Gordon, and Brittanica sat in their baby seats.

ZIIIIIIING!

Three rattles sailed through the air like golden arrows. Dil's flew straight and true, making a perfect arc in the sunbeams that streamed down from the high windows.

It flew toward Mr. Carlssen, who had dashed away to make arrangements for the next event, and hit the bill of his cap.

"Oh, Tommy, Dil won!" said Chuckie to his friend.

"Yeah, that's great," said Tommy with a slight catch in his voice. "Now my parents can take him home with them."

Tommy swallowed hard and looked over at the rest of his family, happily celebrating.

"Okay, listen! Now we will play BASKETBALL!" bellowed Carlssen. "This to be followed by Wee Li'l Walker, Tot Trot, Crib Climb, and then, for the grand finale, IRON BABE!"

Tommy looked over at Dil, who was in their mother's arms. Dil waved to his older brother.

Tommy looked over at Chuckie, who had taken off his glasses and was chewing on them. Phil and Lil were over at the basketball area, staring anxiously at Edie and Petey, who were helping each other stretch out.

The noise level in the room was growing louder by the minute. Tommy looked over at his father. Stu was arguing with Walter's dad, who was holding up a Binky and shouting at him. Betty and Howard were talking heatedly to Edie and Petey's parents.

Brittanica had gotten ahold of Mr. Carlssen's whistle and was blowing on it. Mr. Carlssen was waving his arms wildly, running through the room and yelling, "Win! Win! Win!" with a frenzied look in his eyes.

Suddenly Tommy felt someone clutch his shirt with clammy hands. It was Bubba.

"Tommy, this isn't any fun!" he whimpered. "I don't like that Mr. Carlssen. I don't like my mom and dad yelling all the time."

Victor walked over. "I wanna go splash in the baby pool. I don't wanna do this Limpings stuff."

At the basketball court, Phil, Lil, Edie, and Petey set down their ball and went to where the others were. "We don't wanna do any more yump shots," said Lil. "We wanna go eat some finger paint," she said.

Tommy watched Walter jump off the minitrampoline. A few cracks fanned out from where his feet hit the floor, but Walter didn't notice. He sat down and began trying to tug off the number taped to his back.

"My tummy hurts," whimpered Chuckie.

All the babies were looking at Tommy. "Well . . . guys . . ." he said slowly. He looked around at the parents. "A baby's

gotta do what a baby's gotta do. And I can only think of one thing to do right now. WAAAAAAAAAH!"

As soon as Tommy burst into tears, Bubba did too. So did Victor, Walter, Phil, Lil, Chuckie, and the rest of the babies. Soon the entire room was filled with the sound of wailing babies.

The parents stopped racing around. They ran over to their babies. "Tommy!" said Stu. "Pull yourself together, son! You have a race to run!" Then he stopped himself. He picked up Tommy and patted his back. He looked over at Didi.

"Oh, Stu, how silly we've been behaving!" said Didi.

Stu held Tommy tightly and nodded guiltily. "We sure have, hon," he said.

Bubbles came over to Stu and Didi, carrying Bubba. Klondike joined them, holding Walter. "I say we bag this Baby

Olympics!" bellowed Bubbles. Klondike nodded vigorously.

"Let's take our kids for a swim in the kiddie pool!" suggested Donna Donovan, who was holding a snuffling Petey in her arms.

"Great idea!" said Betty. Everyone left the exercise area except for Mr. Carlssen, who stared at the now-empty room in complete astonishment.

Chapter 8

It was a few days later. Stu sighed contentedly and looked over toward the kiddie pool, where Tommy, Chuckie, Phil, Lil, and several other babies were splashing around happily.

Cindy sat in the lifeguard chair, chatting on her phone as she watched the kids.

"It sure is relaxing around here since Carlssen has been moved over to dining services," Stu said to Didi.

Just then Mr. Carlssen came out to the pool area. He was dressed as Little Red Riding Hood and carried a big basket full of vegetables and dip. After glumly setting it down, he retreated quickly to the kitchen.

Suddenly Didi jumped up. "Mustn't be late! I'm due for a seaweed wrap with Betty before our stretch 'n' burn 'n' tone 'n' trim class!" she said. "Will you watch Dil, Stu? Thanks. I'll see you at supper!" And she dashed off to find Betty.

Stu looked at his watch. "Whoops, almost forgot! I've got a hot-oil heel massage. Come on, Dil." He hauled himself from the lounge chair, picked up Dil, and headed for the spa area.

In the pool Chuckie chucked a ball to Bubba, who gurgled happily and bopped it toward Victor. Victor flipped it to

Walter, whose gentle tap sent it sailing over the palm trees and onto the beach.

"Oops," grinned Walter sheepishly. The other babies giggled.

"I haven't seen the Big Bad Wolf," Chuckie said to Tommy. "Mr. Snarlssen must have screaded it away."

He grinned and added, "This bacation turned out okay after all, Tommy!"

"Yeah, Chuckie," Tommy agreed. He leaned back on his inflatable duck and sighed. "Like I always say, babies just wanna have fun."

About the Author

Sarah Willson has written more than eighty children's books, many of them about the Rugrats! She has been a newspaper cartoonist, and once played semiprofessional basketball. She lives in Connecticut with her husband, three small children, and two large cats.

Sarah is a big sports fan, and likes to write about sports in her stories whenever she can. And her children love the fact that they can have a real basketball hoop in their bedroom!